Metaphysics, Truth and St. Thomas Aquinas

Donald G. Boland

En Route Books and Media, LLC
Saint Louis, MO USA

⊕ENROUTE
Make the time

En Route Books and Media, LLC

5705 Rhodes Avenue

St. Louis, MO 63109

Contact us at **contact@enroutebooksandmedia.com**

Cover Credit: Sebastian Mahfood conjoining images from Bartolomé Esteban Murillo's Santo Tomás de Aquino (1650) and Raffaello Sanzio da Urbino's The School of Athens (1511).

ISBN-13: 979-8-88870-091-4

Library of Congress Control Number: 2023946405

Special thanks to Frank Calneggia for his editing of this book.

Dedicated

to

Saint Karol Wojtyła
Pope John Paul II

Who acutely saw the modern turn away from using the human mind to know the truth about reality to using it to reflect upon itself, and its limitations.

Recentior philosophia, omittens suas perquisitiones in ipsum "esse" dirigere, opus suum in cognitionibus hominum collocavit. Non ergo extulit facultatem quae homini data est veritatis cognoscendae, sed extollere eius limites maluit et condiciones.

Fides et ratio n. 5

"Abandoning the investigation of being, modern philosophical research has concentrated instead upon human knowing. Rather than make use of the human capacity to know the truth, modern philosophy has preferred to accentuate the ways in which this capacity is limited and conditioned."

Quotations

"The mind of man when it is engaged in a sincere search for truths, will never light on one which contradicts the truths it has already ascertained. The Christian will weigh the latest fancy carefully, making sure that he does not lose hold of the truth already in his possession or contaminate it in any way, with great danger and perhaps great loss to the Faith itself."

Pope Pius XII, *Humani Generis*, 12th August 1950

"Since the modern world began in the sixteenth century, nobody's system of philosophy has really corresponded to everybody's sense of reality: to what, if left to themselves, common men would call common sense. Each started with a paradox: a peculiar point of view demanding the sacrifice of what they would call a sane point of view. That is the one thing common to Hobbes and Hegel, to Kant and Bergson to Berkeley and William James. A man had to believe something that no normal man would believe, if it were suddenly propounded to his simplicity; as that law is above right, or right is outside reason, or things are only as we think them, or everything is relative to a reality that is not there. The modern philosopher claims, like a sort of confidence man, that if once we will grant him this, the rest will be easy; he will straighten out the world, if once he is allowed to give this one twist to the mind.

"Against all this the philosophy of St. Thomas stands founded on the universal common conviction that eggs are eggs. The Hegelian may say that an egg is really a hen, because it is a part of an endless process of Becoming; the Berkeleian may hold that poached eggs only exist as a dream exists; since it is quite as easy to call the dream the cause of the eggs as the eggs the cause of the dream; the Pragmatist may believe that we get the best out of scrambled eggs by forgetting that they ever were eggs, and only remembering the scramble. But no pupil of St. Thomas needs to addle his brains in order adequately to addle his eggs; to put his head at any peculiar angle in looking at eggs, or squinting at eggs, or winking the other eye in order to see a new simplification of eggs. The Thomist stands in the broad daylight of the brotherhood of men, in their common consciousness that eggs are not hens or dreams or mere practical assumptions; but things attested by the Authority of the Senses, which is from God.

"Thus, Aquinas insists very profoundly but very practically, that there instantly enters, with this idea of affirmation [of being/*ens*] the idea of contradiction. It is instantly apparent, even to the child, that there cannot be both affirmation and contradiction. Whatever you call the thing he sees, a moon or a mirage or a sensation or a state of consciousness, when he sees it, he knows it is not true that he does not see it. Or whatever you call what he is supposed to be doing, seeing or dreaming or being conscious of an impression, he knows that if he is doing it, it is a lie to say he is not doing it. Therefore there has already entered something beyond even the first fact of being; there follows it like its shadow the first fundamental creed or commandment, that a thing cannot be and not be. Henceforth, in common or popular language, there is a false and true."

G. K. Chesterton, *Saint Thomas Aquinas.*

"'In a universe containing millions of planets,' reasoned Haldane, 'is it not inevitable that life should appear on at least one of them?' 'Sir,' replied Knox, 'if Scotland Yard found a body in your cabin trunk, would you tell them: There are millions of trunks in the world; surely one of them must contain a body? I think they would still want to know who put it there'."

"It is so stupid of modern civilization to have given up believing in the devil when he is the only explanation of it."

Ronald Knox (1888-1957) was engaged in a theological discussion with scientist John Scott Haldane.

Table of Contents

Preface

Under normal circumstances the subject matter of this book would be the first treated in the study of Metaphysics, or natural wisdom. If one looks at Aristotle's *Metaphysics* one finds that after laying down some preliminary matters, and considering the views of others according to his usual practice and laying down a full list of the questions to be considered, he deals with the defence of the most fundamental principle of all, that of non-contradiction (Book Four).

What we need to notice here is that, after considering (dialectically) all the various aspects of questions and difficulties involved, Aristotle goes on to definitively resolve (analytically) the difficulties that underlie seeing the certainty of the principle of non-contradiction. There is no room left for doubt as to its universal validity and truth. Aristotle does not allow for any undermining of certainty of the other basic metaphysical principles, since they can all be defended apodictically, not directly but indirectly by proof *per impossibile* or *ad absurdum*.

So it is that, when confronted with the expressed position of Heraclitus, who denied the principle of non-contradiction, Aristotle provides his famous statement that "what a person says is not necessarily what he thinks", making the point that it is a form of self-deception, and deception of others, to propose that one can honestly adhere to the opposite of the principle of non-contradiction.

This order of absolutely certain principles is common to all sciences and so to deny or doubt them undermines not only Metaphysics but also every other science, not only theoretical, such as Mathematics and the Natural Sciences, but also practical, such as the three ethical sciences (and their prudences) and all the technical sciences and arts. As we have expounded upon, *longe et profunde*, this is the fate that has overtaken the modern mind, more than coincidentally with the rejection of the divine authority of the Catholic Church. The mental collapse, which has marked the "progress" of science in modern times, is rooted in a moral one.

This mental mistake finds its acme (or nadir) in the denial of the first principle of the human intellect. For, the principle is the expression of the most fundamental act of judgment, which is the most perfect act of the intellect. To err in principle Aristotle says is to err incorrigibly. For, there is no "criterion" possible to be had whereby to correct it. It will be seen that the discussion of Metaphysics from this aspect is in the language of the Greek word for judgement, *crisis*. As we shall see, the modern discussion indulges in this language, but has no way of knowing what it really means. Like Heraclitus, having denied the first principle of judging, all their subsequent assertions and denials are verbal only, even to the point of being verbose, and have to be accounted in truth as no more than the irrational cackle of chooks.

However, for one living in the modern age, whilst having to confirm Aristotle's defence in classical times we have the additional task of addressing the problems that have been thrown up with a vehemence that can only be accounted for by reference to the rejection of divine authority after its manifestation in Christ and his Church. This will be the motivation in the philosophy underlying the modern promotion of a new vision of science without wisdom. It could not but end in the breakdown of rationality not only in morals but also in the very understanding of reality.

However, though we should not forget the connection with a moral cause, following a loss of Faith, we are here concerned directly with the question of truth in its own theoretical terms, that is, metaphysically. There are causes of the difficulties and doubts that arise from the nature of the problem itself which Aristotle treats of in a manner that reminds one of Aquinas's generosity of spirit and fair mindedness in dealing with his "opponents" on such basic questions. In this regard there is much that can be applied to the difficulties and doubts of modern philosophers. But, as may be appreciated, the treatment of the modern problem has its own peculiar features. Of necessity, this makes for a much lengthier treatment of the subject matter as it is presented in modern times.

Thus, we divide this our treatment of Metaphysics (called Defensive) into two parts. We first take a look at how Aristotle defends the principle of non-contradiction. This we will do as briefly as we can, with the help of St. Thomas's commentary on Book Four of the *Metaphysics,* where we will focus on the first metaphysical principle itself and Aristotle's treatment of the causes that prompted the ancients to deny or doubt it.

In the second part we will examine the course of treatment of human knowledge and the problems raised with regard to its truth and certainty, which in essence can be reduced to a denial, verbal only as we have noted, of this fundamental principle. There are many causes of this that we need to examine, some of which coincide with ones considered by Aristotle, but the main ones we are interested in are peculiar to the condition of the human mind after the revolt from reason that inevitably followed the rejection of Christian Faith and the divine authority of Christ's Church.

The proper object of the discussion is human knowledge and specifically intellectual and rational knowledge, and the central question is that of truth. That has to be settled, as it was by Aristotle, before we can move on to engage in the proper study of being (Ontology). The examination of the defence done by Aristotle is not in itself a lengthy and laborious task. In modern times it has been made so by a redefinition of science to exclude natural wisdom (and practical wisdom).

Let us, however, first deal with the defence of the truth of our human knowledge, which finds its perfect human expression in the fourth book of Aristotle's *Metaphysics*.

Part 1

Chapter 1

Every other kind of our knowledge and use of the word "truth" hangs upon us getting a proper understanding of the principle of non-contradiction. Knowledge and truth are found in the other acts of human knowing, even to the lowest level of sense, but with a much-diminished meaning.

In order to appreciate this let us survey the nature and division of human knowledge. This depends upon a proper understanding of two sciences that are closely allied to Metaphysics, one which we have already dealt with on Psychology in our book entitled "Psychology Science and Saint Thomas Aquinas", and the other on Logic, which we will deal with in the book immediately following this one, which will be entitled "Logic, Science and Saint Thomas Aquinas".

In the normal order of study, as explained by St. Thomas, Logic comes well before Metaphysics. Indeed, it is the first to be dealt with in the order of study of philosophy and science. But, for reasons we have already given, taking into account the modern situation, we have chosen another order. In regard to what we are wishing to bring out here, we need to anticipate what is brought out more fully in Logic. However, let us first recapitulate some of what we have said in Psychology.

Modern philosophers and scientists, because of their crass materialism, generally cannot get off first base in this study. For, let alone not having any understanding of that level of human knowledge that is understanding, they do not even begin to understand the most elementary form of life and therefore what is meant by soul (*psyche*) as the intrinsic principle of life in living things. We go into the implications of this materialist way of explanation, combined with a notion of form that is based in mathematics, in our last book in this series "Natural Philosophy, Modern Science and St. Thomas Aquinas". So we will only go briefly here into the deficiencies of modern thinking based in a profound ignorance of human psychology.

But we cannot proceed without interposing some comments on a problem we face all the time in all aspects of the discussion of the philosophy of Aristotle and Aquinas even where one might expect some adherence to accuracy and faithfulness to their thought in English translation. We quote three paragraphs of a highly respected English translation right at the beginning of Book Four with the Latin given, and the relevant words put in bold, so as to show how poorly the translator performs his most important task.

"529. In the preceding book the Philosopher proceeded to treat **dialectically** the things which ought to be considered in this science. Here he begins to proceed **demonstratively** by **establishing** the **true answer** to those questions which have been **raised and argued dialectically**."

*In praecedenti libro philosophus **disputative** processit de illis, quae debent in hac scientia considerari: hic incipit procedere demonstrative determinando **veritatem** quaestionum **prius motarum et disputatarum**.*

One will notice firstly that *disputative* is translated by "dialectically". St. Thomas uses the word "dialectic" in the strict Aristotelian sense in every part of his work and especially in this subject area. The two words are close in meaning. But for his own reasons Aquinas chooses to use "disputatively". Why does the translator not use this obvious equivalent – is he trying to display his ability to read the mind of Aquinas? This annoying trait of translators to go by the principle "what is near enough is good enough" is all over the place in "interpreting" what Aquinas means rather than translating what he says.

But, much worse is to come. In the very second sentence we have "establishing" (a word used by builders) used for *determinendo* and "true answer" for *veritatitem* (the truth) and "argued dialectically" for disputedly; *prius* just does not get translated. For the modern mind, a "true answer" is not quite the same as "the truth" and carries the stink of scepticism, implying an answer that is true according to Aristotle's opinion. The translator no doubt learnt in his first year of philosophy in a modern university or seminary that philosophy is all about opinion – there is no absolute truth. This will come out starkly in the translation of the third paragraph, which we give after the second paragraph which shows only how the use of dialectically, which incidentally is to do with opinions, is ingrained.

"In the preceding book he **treated dialectically** both the things which pertain to the method of this science, namely, those to which the consideration of this science extends, as well as those which fall under the consideration of this science. And because it is first necessary to know the method of a science before proceeding to consider the things with which it deals, as was explained in Book II (335), this part is therefore divided into two members. First, he speaks of the things which this science considers; and second (749), of those which fall under its consideration. He does this in Book V ("In one sense the term principle").”

*Fuit autem in praecedenti libro **disputatum** tam de his quae pertinent ad modum huius scientiae, scilicet ad quae se extendit huius scientiae consideratio, quam etiam de his quae sub consideratione huius scientiae cadunt. Et quia prius oportet cognoscere modum scientiae quam procedere in scientia ad ea consideranda de quibus est scientia, ut in secundo libro dictum est: ideo dividitur haec pars in duas. Primo dicit de quibus est consideratio huius scientiae. Secundo dicit de rebus quae sub consideratione huius scientiae cadunt, in quinto libro, ibi, principium dicitur aliud quidem et cetera.*

So let us look at how what Aquinas says about Aristotle solving the problem he is considering gets diluted to "answering", namely, giving his opinion. So we have merely by bad translation the reader set up to treat philosophy (wisdom), and science consequently, as merely a matter of opinion. Why does the secularist education system (installed also in Catholic institutions) need professors who are skilled in the art of dialectic/sophistry when the translators have already done the scepticism work for them?

"The first part is divided into two members. First, he establishes what **the subject matter** of this science is. Second (534), he proceeds **to answer the questions raised** in the preceding book about the things which this science considers ("The term be-ing")."

*Prima in duas. Primo subiectum stabilit huius scientiae. Secun-do procedit ad **solvendum** quaestiones **motas** in libro praecedenti de consideratione huius scientiae, ibi, ens autem multis.*

That is just a taste of the difficulty put in one's way in this most critical of subject matters for both the understanding of Ar-istotle's thought and the defence of Metaphysics in the modern morass. But we must proceed as best we can. There is no point in picking up every mistranslation but we will try to notice the most egregious ones.

As for the Psychology we need to get straight, we need to first get a correct understanding of the difference between the living and the non-living if we are to make any progress in this subject matter. For, knowledge is a form of life, obviously a higher form. So we can then go on to distinguish the living into the knowing and the non-knowing, which comes out clearly in the difference between plants and animals. Finally, we will come to distinguish the knowing into the being that knows by sense knowledge and the other that knows by intellectual/ rational knowledge.

What will complicate matters is the fact that the human being exists and operates on all three levels of life. Thus it is fundamen-tal that we first understand the basis of the difference between the living and the non-living, which we will soon see lies in the difference between immanent and transitive activity.

All beings have activity, which in bodies is called motion, though going by external appearances we commonly differentiate between non-living things as active, like fire, and inactive like rocks. The ancients tended to speak in these terms (even Aristotle) but one thing that modern science has revealed is that even rocks are made up of parts in constant motion and act on "their environment".

But we are more directly interested in the difference between living and non-living activity in terms of the difference between immanent and transitive activity. One has only to step on a rat thinking it is a rock. The gap between living things and non-living still astounds scientists. Aristotle will explain it as a new form of being, infinitely superior to what is immediately below it, not a matter of degree, nor even specific, but generic. We may describe an electric wire as "live". But we are aware that we are speaking metaphorically – no different from calling someone a "live wire".

This brings out something we wish to focus on in the use of the distinction between immanent and transitive activity, as it is the fundamental difference between the living and the non-living. The living thing can move itself; the non-living can only move something other than itself (immanent = remains within, transitive = goes over). But we are deceived sometimes where the two kinds of activity are alike in some way, somewhat like equating a fire "feeding" on dry grass as if it were something alive like a herd of horses.

What we will notice with modern thought since Descartes is that the distinction between immanence and transitivity gets mixed up with what is internal to the human mind and what is external and it is the former that comes to be called immanent. By a process of distortion of thought and language originating in Descartes all bodily activity outside "mind" gets reduced not just to transitive activity but even to pure passivity, putting external reality as he does in terms of pure extension.

Not only does this confuse immanent activity with activity itself, but also it empties bodies of their physical qualities and activities and they are dealt with as empirio-mathematical "entities" in the newly arising Newtonian Physics. But we will come to that shortly.

It is the more fundamental distortion in the notion of life (and consequently knowledge) that concerns us here. It results in the rubbing out of the distinction between immanent activity and transitive activity as it applies throughout the whole range of living bodily life, from plants nourishing themselves by the vital activity of assimilating material things as food, to animals informing themselves of objects by vitally/cognitively assimilating the forms of sensible things. The Cartesians and empiricists made a horrible mess of this philosophically and modern thought from Kant to the present day has not recovered.

The matter is complicated by the fact that in bodily life immanent activity does not act alone but needs to use the lower transitive activity of other bodies to accomplish its ends. This is most evident in the way a plant nourishes itself not by eating its own body as it were but by drawing on the material goodness in minerals etc. Of necessity this involves the destruction or loss of natural form of the materials used. But it also involves some transitive activity of the materials consumed, called chemical in modern scientific language. This plant-like vital activity is also present in the higher forms of life in animal and human bodies.

So, though it may appear that the food actively nourishes the living body, in truth this non vital activity acts instrumentally, controlled by the living – try feeding hay to a dead horse. Thus we have to be careful with properly distinguishing the Latin derived words, nourisher (*nutriens*), nourished (*nouritum*) and nourishment (*nutrimentum*). The horse nourishes itself (is both the nourisher and nourished) from the hay (nutriment). It is of little consequence that ordinary language does not pay much attention to these fine distinctions, but modern biology, because of its materialist philosophical underpinning, simply ignores them, treating the whole process as a complex of transitive actions and "reactions".

The new notion of science has thus destroyed our knowledge and appreciation of the natural forms and their proper beauties in respect of all the diverse levels of living things in the physical world. It is a blank and even grim picture of nature that modern science has substituted. But, fortuitously, in a way that we have explained in our previous books, it produced an increase in control of nature and the production of great material wealth (capital) – for some. The connection with the rise of the modern politico-economic system of Capitalism/ Proletarianism has been explained in our earlier books.

As to what was lost by the blurring of lines of distinction in the natural world so far as the various kinds of life is concerned we simply refer the reader to our book "Psychology, Science and Saint Thomas Aquinas". By a sleight of hand, contrary to Descartes's concept of things outside the mind as purely inactive, the empirical/ material side of modern science, come through Francis Bacon, converts all bodily activity (all human bodily activity being conceived in the same terms) into transitive activity, thereby eliminating the very notion of immanent activity. The modern scientist is not concerned about the contradiction that this involves, nor with the fact that the distinct realities of life, and knowledge, remain unintelligible in modern science.

There is one consequence of the distortion of the notion of immanence that has however carried through from Cartesian rationalism, that has penetrated so deeply into modern consciousness that it has affected not only the thought and language use of modern philosophers and scientists, but also of those who wish to resist its erroneousness and remain faithful to the "perennial philosophy" come down into Christian and Catholic life and thinking from Aquinas. Certainly, the change in language use inaugurated by Descartes (a devout Catholic) with regard to the relation between subject and object has taken over in large degree that belonging to Aristotle's way of talking about subject generally and, where relevant, about objectivity.

We have to remember that "subject" simply means what is "thrown under" (*sub-iectum*) whereas "object" means "thrown against" (*ob iectum*). The first word has a familiar significance in the context of human speech and intellectual knowledge with particular reference to the proposition or sentence (what is

thrown under a predicate). But it has a more fundamental significance when being is taken in the real (outside the propositional
form within the mind). Here it stands for substance as the primary kind of real being (what stands under accidents). The "mind"
or human person is only one kind of substance, if the highest in
the natural order – that which is most perfect as St. Thomas puts
it. However, it is not only human beings with their spiritual substantial forms and intellectual powers or "minds" that are "subjects" but all beings non-living and living, non-knowing and
knowing, non "thinking" and rational are subjects in this metaphysical sense.

One may begin to appreciate the distance between the thinking of moderns and that of Aristotle and Aquinas purely from the
confusion of concepts in regard to the notions of subject and object. All sorts of fundamental distinctions go necessarily and radically awry. It is no wonder that the various attempts of modern
philosophers who try to explain modern science take them off in
every direction and end up in one unholy mess of contradictions
within each new philosophy and between them all. As we will see,
most even revel in their denial of the principle of non-
contradiction. Maritain described Hegel's dialectical idealism as a
murderous system of thought. Marx's conversion of it into a
praxis, which he called dialectical materialism, made it all too
true that it was diabolically so.

We do not go into here the distortion in the use of the word
"immanent" which now becomes opposed to "transcendent" and
we have the nonsensical employment of these words in modern

sociology where "immanent " is applied to the system of modern science as locked into our regard for material things as the only reality. It is called immanent as referring to what fills the human mind now closed to anything "transcending" it. Charles Taylor's book "A Secular Age" is a prime example of trying to employ this distorted language in the cause of religion.

There are therefore all sorts of false trails and dead ends that the modern mind engages on following the inversion of terms that has resulted from what Pope Saint John Paul II, in *Fides et ratio n. 5*, described as "Abandoning the investigation of being, modern philosophical research has concentrated instead upon human knowing. Rather than make use of the human capacity to know the truth, modern philosophy has preferred to accentuate the ways in which this capacity is limited and conditioned."

The pope goes on to describe the general effect of this turning away from the real world in which we live, and the God who has created it, to a world within ourselves (note the moral implications) that we imagine is our own creation. This is the basic reason why the modern mind has got the notions of "subject" and "object" upside down but also is not only incapable of acknowledging the simple truth of the principle of non-contradiction.

"This has given rise to different forms of agnosticism and relativism which have led philosophical research to lose its way in the shifting sands of widespread scepticism. Recent times have seen the rise to prominence of various doctrines which tend to devalue even the truths which had been judged certain. A legitimate plurality of positions has yielded to an undifferentiated pluralism, based upon the assumption that all positions are equally valid, which is one of today's most widespread symptoms of the lack of confidence in truth. Even certain conceptions of life coming from the East betray this lack of confidence, denying truth its exclusive character and assuming that truth reveals itself equally in different doctrines, even if they contradict one another. On this understanding, everything is reduced to opinion; and there is a sense of being adrift. While, on the one hand, philosophical thinking has succeeded in coming closer to the reality of human life and its forms of expression, it has also tended to pursue issues—existential, hermeneutical or linguistic—which ignore the radical question of the truth about personal existence, about being and about God. Hence we see among the men and women of our time, and not just in some philosophers, attitudes of widespread distrust of the human being's great capacity for knowledge. With a false modesty, people rest content with partial and provisional truths, no longer seeking to ask radical questions about the meaning and ultimate foundation of human, personal and social existence. In short, the hope that philosophy might be able to provide definitive answers to these questions has dwindled." (F & R, n. 5)

This should suffice to explain how the inversion of terms of "subject" and "object" became so embedded because of a misunderstanding of Human Psychology. However, we have already noted how a misunderstanding of Logic contributed to the inversion of the use of these terms. We will go more into this in the next book on Logic, but will make some short comments here.

Human understanding depends upon two sources, the action of external things whereby their forms are received into the intellect and the superior internal activity of the agent intellect, which is needed to render these forms actually intelligible so as able to be received into the potential or receiving intellect. We have already discussed how this activity of the agent intellect is compared to light but it is also an activity of abstraction of the intelligible content of a natural form (say of horse) from sense impressions or images first had.

This is more fully elaborated upon in the study of Human Psychology. But this abstraction means that the form as received in the human intellect is in a different condition from what it is in the senses. This we express by saying that the form as sensed as singular or individual whereas on reception in the intellect it acquires the condition of universality. The horse that is sensed or imagined is the same in essence as this horse but understood is referable to every horse or thing of the same nature or essence. It is the one nature that is sayable of all individuals (*unum versus alia*).

This universal property, however, is something that is added to the abstract form in mind by the mind. Hence, it is a logical relation, which as such does not exist outside the mind but only as a mental relation added to the concept in the mind.

Nonetheless, the object or content of the concept is not for that a mental or logical construct. It is the same form (horse) existing outside the mind, and known by the intellect, but not according to the conditions of its individual existence. We have to be careful to distinguish between the two parts of the concept, the abstract object and its universal condition in the mind. The second part is necessarily a mental addition; the first however is not. Indeed, it is initially a real form that informs the human intellect so that it comes to be by knowledge everything that belongs to its world.

These two distinct parts of the concept and proposition tend to get mixed up not only in modern times but also throughout the history of Logic and Metaphysics. Plato's philosophy is the classic case in this regard. Aristotle therefore distinguishes Formal Logic, which deals with the logical relations had in the mind only, from the "material" content of what is dealt with under the logical forms, firstly with what is common to the object of the concept, but then more elaborated upon in the "matter" of propositions and argumentations. Thus, the content part of what is in the mind is to do primarily which such forms of real things as horses.

This is where the question of truth (conformity between thought and thing) comes in; it is focused on the content of, or object in, the concept. But then the mind has to bring in all sorts of mental entities as instruments for understanding things. Such are purely logical products of negations (even the concept of nothing) and privations (as the concept of evil). These are all purely mental "beings" but treated, as Aristotle explains, as the content of our concepts etc. This is what the scholastics intended by pure objects. They are in the mind and from the mind as secondary and instrumental "entities", but not for that to be accounted of negligible significance in the work of science. Just consider, for instance, how Mathematics would fare without the use of the square root of minus one. We may appreciate then how the relation between Logic and Metaphysics, and also the other sciences of the real is quite complex.

We have to proceed very carefully therefore so as not to distort our understanding not only of Logic but also of Metaphysics and the other sciences of the real, which depend upon Logic in all sorts of ways. We will just instance one part of Logic where the subject of the statement or proposition is say evil, that does not refer to any real form of being, or substance in things, but is treated as a substantive in a sentence or statement.

Take the famous proposition in morals: "good is from an integrating cause, whilst evil is from whatsoever defect". Here we have a mixing of two kinds of subjects in propositions, one that is founded in the reality of good, the other in the "unreality" of evil. Both are true statements, but in the one case the truth is based in thing. In the other the truth means to refer to what is outside the mind, as a lack, but in order to do so has to speak of the privation as if it were a positive form of being.

Aristotle had already discussed the analogy of being and pointed out that the being (IS) of the proposition is being in a secondary sense. There is a possible confusion here, for the "is" of the proposition has two modes of signification. It may signify the real existence of the thing as when we say: "a dog bit the child". This again can signify from experience as when I see the dog bite the child or from reasoning as when a medico deduces the proposition from the examination of the nature of the bite. The second of these (by mode of conclusion) differs from the first radically, but both refer to a real event.

Nonetheless, it does not constitute what Aristotle called the "is" of the proposition, as being purely in a secondary sense. This is where the object of the concept and the subject of the proposition is a negation or privation, something simply constructed in the mind for the sake of thinking and speaking about things. Here we have a case of the being of a proposition constituting an analogous use of being, in a secondary sense, as explained above.

Here we have to be most careful, especially in dealing with analogy with regard to God. There is a place where St. Thomas answers a question about our knowledge of the existence of God where he seems to say that what we prove is nothing real about God, but are concluding to a truth that is a propositional truth only. This can be misleading. For, what we intend to prove is the real existence of God, not from direct experience but rather as a deduction from sensible evidence, as we have illustrated with the case of the dog bite. The conclusion is only known by means of and in terms of the effects experienced.

Yet, even here we need to carefully note the uniqueness of our conclusion. For the nature of the dog bite is proportional to its canine nature, which we do otherwise have proper knowledge of. We cannot know anything of God, his essence or existence, except in terms of what is not God but his effects, which are totally disproportionate to God. Naturally, the Creator remains an unknown God even with our being certain of his existence and what he necessarily is as the cause of being, which is mainly in negative terms.

So, we have to be careful in referring to the being of the proposition as not the same as real being. It does as such only signify the union of predicate and subject in the mind, but it is not to be thought that the content is necessarily unreal as is the case when we speak about negations and privations. There are two significations of the "is" of the proposition. In the one case, as when we affirm that the horse exists, we are using the "is" as predicate, indeed the supreme predicate signifying real existence. Kant got mixed up here. When we say the horse is an animal the "is" unites its essence to the subject horse, whether any actual horse exists or not. But the nature of horse is real. The distinction here is between existence and essence, not to be confused with real and purely mental existence.

But the further treatment of these distinctions of a logical kind can be left to the next book. What we want to bring out here is how the understanding of what is subjective and objective has been affected by an undue focus on logical matters. This turns our attention inward, upon ourselves, and the operations of our minds.

It is well known that even before Descartes, in late scholasticism, there was a turn to an excessive focus on Logic. This prepared the way for the Cartesian "angelism". It gave the impression of a turn to the more spiritual side of human life but it undermined this by cutting human life from the real world and so damaging its sense of dependence upon God as Creator, as we have seen explained by Pope Benedict XVI in our previous book "Thomas of the Creator".

With Descartes the meaning of subject was changed to signifying exclusively the human person and that without its metaphysical support as substance. We will come back to this after going over Aristotle's treatment of the first principle of the human intellect, the principle of non-contradiction, which is the judgment that uses the concept of being. It is not a merely propositional or logical truth but one that is founded in the world of reality and substance. It is this notion of subject as substance, a metaphysical reality, that we need to restore.

The treatment of the principle of non-contradiction St. Thomas says is what Aristotle is principally concerned with having determined that Metaphysics is properly concerned with defending first principles as well as expounding upon first concepts such as being and unity. Here unfortunately we must protest once more against the failure of the English translator to render the right sense of the Latin.

It is not just another instance of poverty of understanding of the ordinary meaning of the Latin words used; it is a positive (no doubt ignorant) mistranslation that distorts the whole sense of the passage. I would go so far to say that it undermines the understanding by the English reader of the whole of Book Four if not of the whole of Aristotle's work on Metaphysics.

It is telling that the translator translates *principaliter* by "particularly" in the sub-heading "helpfully" given, the word changed to "chiefly" (a weak form of "principally") in the first sentence of the commentary. But, the use of "particularly" gives the whole game away. It is a favourite term used by English speaking philosophers who cannot think in any way except univocally. A cat is a particular species of animal; no one would suggest it is the principal kind of animal, even if the lion is the king (chief) of the jungle.

So we have the metaphysical language mangled from the start. St. Thomas is highlighting the fact of the stark prominence of the principle of non-contradiction in Aristotle's treatment of first principles. When you add to that that it is the principal work of the act of judgment that is the most perfect act of intellect you may get some idea of how fundamental it is to the certainty of our human knowledge. Aristotle lays out its conditions. The Latin is also given and words highlighted so that the reader may get some idea of how the strong Latin expressions are watered down, We give only one example where "making a mistake" translates for *mentiri,* which means to be deceived and even lied to. We have seen how Aristotle declared that it must amount to self-deception even in the case of the most celebrated of philosophers.

The translator does his own highlighting to little effect, it being noteworthy that he does not highlight the second condition, as this would offend the first condition of modern science.

Deinde cum dicit et firmissimum hic ostendit quid sit firmissimum sive certissimum principium: et circa hoc duo facit. Primo dicit quae sunt conditiones certissimi principii. Deinde adaptat eas uni principio, ibi, quid vero sit et cetera.

"Then he shows what the firmest or most certain principle is; and in regard to this he does two things. First, he states the conditions for the most certain principle; and then (600) he shows how they fit a single principle ("And let us")."

Ponit ergo primo, tres conditiones firmissimi principii. Prima est, quod circa **hoc non possit aliquis mentiri**, *sive errare. Et hoc patet, quia cum homines non decipiuntur nisi circa ea quae ignorant: ideo circa quod non potest aliquis decipi, oportet esse notissimum.*

"He accordingly gives, first, the three conditions for the firmest principle. (1) The first is that **no one can make a mistake** or be in error regarding it. And this is evident because, since men make mistakes only about those things which they do not know, then that principle about which no one can be mistaken must be the one which is best known."

Secunda conditio est ut sit non conditionale, idest non propter suppositionem habitum, sicut illa, quae ex quodam condicto ponuntur. Unde alia translatio habet. Et non subiiciantur, idest non subiiciantur ea, quae sunt certissima principia. Et hoc ideo, quia illud, quod necessarium est habere intelligentem quaecumque entium hoc non est conditionale, idest non est suppositum, sed oportet per se esse notum. Et hoc ideo, quia ex quo ipsum est necessarium ad intelligendum quodcumque, oportet quod quilibet qui alia est cognoscens, ipsum cognoscat.

"598. (2) The second condition is that it must "not be hypothetical," i.e., it must not be held as a supposition, as those things which are maintained through some kind of common agreement.

Hence another translation reads "And they should not hold a subordinate place," i.e., those principles which are most certain should not be made dependent on anything else. And this is true, because whatever is necessary for understanding anything at all about being "is not hypothetical," i.e., it is not a supposition but must be self-evident. And this is true because whatever is necessary for understanding anything at all must be known by anyone who knows other things."

Tertia conditio est, ut non acquiratur per demonstrationem, vel alio simili modo; sed adveniat quasi per naturam habenti ipsum, quasi ut naturaliter cognoscatur, et non per acquisitionem. Ex ipso enim lumine naturali intellectus agentis prima principia fiunt cognita, nec acquiruntur per ratiocinationes, sed solum per hoc quod eorum termini innotescunt. Quod quidem fit per hoc, quod a sensibilibus accipitur memoria et a memoria experimentorum et ab experimento illorum terminorum cognitio, quibus cognitis cognoscuntur huiusmodi propositiones communes, quae sunt artium et scientiarum principia.

"599. (3) The third condition is that it is not acquired by demonstration or by any similar method, but it comes in a sense by nature to the one having it inasmuch as it is naturally known and not acquired. For first principles become known through the natural light of the agent intellect, and they are not acquired by any process of reasoning but by having their terms become known. This comes about by reason of the fact that memory is derived from sensible things, experience from memory, and knowledge of those terms from experience. And when they are

known, common propositions of this kind, which are the principles of the arts and sciences, become known."

*Manifestum est ergo quod certissimum principium sive firmis-
simum, tale debet esse, ut circa id non possit errari, et quod non sit
suppositum et quod adveniat naturaliter.*

"Hence it is evident that the most certain or firmest principle
should be such that there can be no error regarding it; that it is
not hypothetical; and that it comes naturally to the one having
it."

In n. 600 St. Thomas sets out the principle itself, which the
translator puts in this way. We were hoping that he could at least
get this right but alas a forlorn hope in the circumstances of his
"education" in philosophy even it would seem in a Catholic and
Dominican school.

"600. Then he indicates the principle to which the above definition applies. He says that it applies to this principle, as the one
which is firmest: it is impossible **for the same attribute both to
belong and not belong to the same subject at the same time**.
And it is necessary to add "in the same respect"; and any other
qualifications that have to be given regarding this principle "to
meet **dialectical** difficulties" must be laid down, since without
these qualifications there would seem to be a contradiction when
there is none."

The Latin is put below with the relevant highlighting. The
principle is a metaphysical one but the translator does his best to
suggest it is a merely logical one (for the moderns mix up the
two, working as they do mostly in Mathematics). Then, not

knowing what *secundum idem* really means, he plays safe and puts the English in inverted commas (a favourite ploy of the ignorant). *Logicas* of course gets translated as "dialectical". We have already commented upon this confusion.

Deinde cum dicit quid vero ostendit cui principio praedicta determinatio conveniat: et dicit, quod huic principio convenit tamquam firmissimo, quod est impossibile **eidem simul inesse et non inesse idem: sed addendum est, et secundum idem**: *et etiam alia sunt determinanda circa hoc principium, quaecumque determinari contingit ad* **logicas** *difficultates, sine quibus videtur contradictio cum non sit.*

Need we go on? It is a rather pointless exercise in standard English translations. There is no hope for the modern Catholic philosopher and theologian if he (or she) does not read and understand Aquinas in Latin. It is not a matter of being expert in the Greek of Aristotle, for without the genial insights of St. Thomas one is more likely to go astray than not. Look at the modern Oxford and Cambridge educated Aristotelians. Even those who also have the advantage of a Thomist background, like Anthony Kenny, cannot but fail to be adversely affected by their immersion in the atmosphere of "Analytical Philosophy" and the presuppositions of modern science.

However, with these warning signals well lit up we will venture a little further with the exposition of Book Four, given that it is so "critical" to the well being of the human mind in its modern situation.

What we should note is the brevity with which Aristotle deals with the first principle itself, its simple statement. This is expressed by St. Thomas in Latin in n. 600 as *quod est impossibile* **eidem simul inesse et non inesse idem: sed addendum est, et secundum idem.** We have criticised the English translation given there. The correct translation is: it is impossible for the same together to be and not be: provided we add according to the same. Unwittingly it seems, the translator gives a translation in n. 605 that differs from that in n. 600 but approaches a correct translation. The one in n. 605 is an almost accurate translation of what St. Thomas has given in Latin, in a more succinct way: *impossibile est esse et non esse simul.* This is translated as: "it is impossible for a thing both to be and not be at the same time". The only problem here is *simul* just means together, and "time" as ordinarily understood applies only to material things. So the reader is left to fall into the modern materialist way of thinking so deeply embedded in his secularist education.

What Aristotle says in his short way, as expounded upon by St. Thomas in nn. 600 to 605, contains all that needs to be said to anyone who understands properly the proposition. But, Aristotle acknowledges that some, including those seriously philosophical, may have difficulty with the certainty of the principle. This he puts down basically to two sources, one outside the mind being the instability from potency or matter in the object of the human intellect, and the other internally from the relative impotency or lack of power in the human intellect. There are many way in which these two sources of difficulty can mislead us into thinking that there may be some uncertainty about our knowledge of things and their causes.

So it is that Aristotle, like a good teacher, spends a lot of time addressing all the sorts of difficulties raised by the natural philosophers on account of the changeableness of the object of our knowledge and by the dialecticians and sophists on account of the contrariety of opinions. As we have noted, the English translator seems to think that any cause of disputation is dialectical, and mixes up as well the two words logical and dialectical.

Just to have some idea of the proportions involved in regard to the principal issue in Book Four, which we generally call the defensive part of Metaphysics, or the justification of the truth of human knowledge, let us note that Aristotle deals with the subject matter in about four chapters in approximately 100 numbered paragraphs (294-402) whilst the commentary of Aquinas occupies 17 lessons in approximately 450 numbered paragraphs (300-748). All that needed to be said is contained in 5 paragraphs of Aquinas's Lesson 6 (600-605).

The first part of Book Four (covered in Lessons 1–5 of Aquinas's commentary) is to do with the first act of the human mind, apprehension, and its product the concept of being, to which Aristotle closely ties that of unity. Even Books 1 to 3, occupied with preliminary considerations of method and the proper subject matter of Metaphysics in terms of the first concept, of being (ens), may be considered on reflection as leading up to the principal consideration of the subject matter of Metaphysics as the product of judgment, or the first proposition, the principle of non-contradiction.

It is important to understand that though the expression of this first principle takes the logical form of a proposition the real subject matter is in the content of this proposition, which is real and metaphysical. The same applies in the case of the first concept, of being. It may take what appears to be the logical form of a universal or genus but its objective reference is to being in the real. Aristotle expressly denies that being is a genus.

The complex nature of objects taken from things outside the mind but dressed with logical properties within the mind causes all sorts of confusion in the particular sciences, but especially in Metaphysics. It is this entanglement that Aristotle tries to sort out with regard to how we know truth.

But, this has to be addressed principally in the act of judgment and too much focus on the concept of being will affect our appreciation of certainty and truth. For, in the human intellect the other two acts of apprehension and reasoning are ultimately ordered to the second, of judgment.

The attempt to confine our grasp of reality to the level of "reason" (*ratio*) can prove sometimes to be an obstacle to our deeper grasp of reality at the level of pure intellection (*intellectus*). These other acts and products of the human mind are necessary aids to achieving truth in its perfect state, but they can also distract us from the main "game". We have often quoted St. Thomas's famous saying: "The aim of philosophy is not to know what many have thought (and said) but how the truth of thing is". This is where Dialectic, which focuses on opinions, can be used to mislead (descending to Sophistic) rather than lead us to make the right judgments, and especially at the higher intellectual level of Metaphysics. Modern philosophy, we may say, mistakes Dialectic for Metaphysics; and modern science mistakes Physics (mixed with Mathematics) for the deepest consideration of the real world.

What we find in modern philosophy and science is that the rejection of Metaphysics has resulted in an exacerbation of these two mistakes. This is something we need to explore more fully in the following chapters of this book. Aristotle shows up the errors and deceptions that are indulged in, and constitute the history of modern philosophy, in his most thorough examination and refutation of them as proposed in ancient times.

He does acknowledge that there is a great deal of difficulty involved in defending the first principle because of the extrinsic causes he refers to. Indeed, the degree of indulgence he shows to those who hold and propose the errors and deceptions he is concerned to refute is remarkable. He says we should be grateful to them in raising these difficulties, for they thereby enable us to better understand the truth by solving them.

However, we do not plan to expound further on what Aristotle and Aquinas have said on all the aspects of the defence of the first principle of non-contradiction. For, their exposition is more than adequate and generally attempts to improve upon them are more of a hindrance than a help.

We shall move on then to the modern treatment of the subject matter, which on account of its complexity will involve a number of chapters. So we begin with our own Chapter Two.

Part 2

Part 2

Chapter 2

It was necessary to begin the study of Metaphysics, as Aristotle did, by settling the question of the truth and certainty of our human knowledge right at its root, as it were. For, if there is no fixity in the foundations of a thing, such as a building, the whole structure cannot stand.

As we have seen, our knowledge is based on having somehow a union with being or things in the midst of which we exist. How this union takes place we have dealt with in our book "Psychology, Science and Saint Thomas Aquinas". In this we saw that at the level of knowledge proper to us as human beings, namely intellectual, there are three acts involved, apprehension, judgment and reasoning. But, in this part of our knowledge, which is concerned with foundations, it is the first two with which we are concerned, together with the products intimately connected to them, concept and proposition.

The first concept is being; the first proposition is the principle of non-contradiction. Though being comes into our intellect in the first act of apprehension in which the mind produces the first concept, it should be remembered that the second act, judgment, is the perfection of the understanding in an intellect. Moreover, truth is first fully had in the judgment.

So it is that Aristotle has put the basis of certainty and truth in the having of the principle of non-contradiction, within which is generated as it were what is in concept in the apprehension of being (*id quod primo cadit in intellectu est ens*). Thus, though the first concept comes before the first proposition, truth blossoms as it were in the first proposition. As Aristotle explains, the principle of non-contradiction is expressed in terms of being.

There are some features of the word 'being' that disclose this relationship. The concept itself (*ens*) is made up of two parts, *essentia* and *esse*, but the name being is taken through reference to *esse* (in contrast to thing, *res*, which is taken through reference to *essentia*.) So it is that within the apprehension itself there is a relation to *esse* or existence, which is fully brought out only in the judgment. Interestingly, "word" (in Latin *verbum*) has the sense of the active part of a proposition fundamentally contained in "is". So, we draw a distinction between being as a noun, and being as a verb.

It is here right at the heart of Metaphysics, as its subject differs from "subject" as applied to all the other sciences, that we have the peculiar overlap between noun and verb, or having as direct object thing (essence) and existence (*esse*). We need to understand, if with difficulty, this peculiarity about the subject matter or formal object of Metaphysics if we are to make some sense of several things that St. Thomas says.

For instance, he does not like to use "abstraction" in the same way as it is used in the particular sciences of Mathematics and Physics, but prefers "separation" when distinguishing the method of Metaphysics. For the intellect separates out all matter when it considers things metaphysically.

This makes for a problem when the first things which we have to consider metaphysically are material. But we can gain some insight into this if we focus on *esse* as the fundamental part of even material things. Also we can begin to understand the root of the difficulties and doubts that plague the mind when we consider the first principle as the foundation of truth in our minds, and as so certain that it cannot really be doubted, let alone denied.

It is from turning our gaze from the firmness of judgment to address the problem from what is a weak spot, as it were, in the concept of being that our mind seems to falter. For we are moving out of the familiar territory of considering all things in terms of *ratio* or essence or thing. *Ratio* applies principally to the act of reasoning, which is meant to complete the truths we know through the principles had by judgment. But, it also apples to the act of apprehension, whose products are preparatory to propositions, and involve "rational" works, such as definitions.

So it is that Aristotle put two sources of our difficulties and doubts, even in the most luminous and clearest of first principles; that is in the two areas of our thinking where reason/*ratio* and reasoning dominate our minds, namely, logic in general and the study of nature. This latter are the natural sciences or natural philosophy, as opposed to metaphysics, but within which we ought also to include mathematics and physico-mathematics.

Thus it is that he deals extensively with the problems raised by the natural philosophers, with whom we can associate Heraclitus, as we can associate modern evolutionists as the (materialist) "philosophers" of the natural world or physical universe.

The second party are the dialecticians and sophists, such as Protagoras, who, desiring to appear wise rather than be wise, for reasons Aristotle gives, deal with "metaphysical" questions treated as matters of opinion. They were prominent in ancient times and are no less so in modern times. Indeed, they abound in the modern universities, because this source of scepticism is fortified by the factor of subjectivism introduced into modern thought by Descartes.

For this reason we can leave the reader to study directly the refutations by Aristotle as masterfully commented upon by Aquinas, of these two sources of deceit and error in ancient times, and from here on consider the modern counterparts. Indeed, this treatment amounts in the main to a study of the history of modern philosophy as affected by the denial of the principle of non-contradiction including to how it impacts on the study of modern science.

Descartes

The study of modern philosophy generally begins with Descartes. The rest of this Chapter will therefore consider his thought as it marks a clear break with the past, in fact something revolutionary in human philosophy and science. Descartes himself wanted his effort to be a clean break with all that had gone before, but only with a view to putting human thinking and action on a firmer foundation, and indeed, as a devout Catholic, so as to provide a surer rational defence of the Faith of the Church to which he belonged.

It is important to understand the social conditions of the time in which he lived. But before we do that we will briefly address his famous "argument" by which he sought to refute the sceptical intellectual climate that had arisen in late mediaeval times. It is put in Latin in these terms: *cogito ergo sum*, which is translated as "I think therefore I am".

This basis of certainty follows in his mind the elimination of all other purported certitudes of human knowledge from the lowest sense level (of touch) to the highest intellectual level, even of Metaphysics as he imagined it. We say: "imagined" because, as a mathematician, Descartes' thinking was locked into his imagination and he did not really think in metaphysical terms, such as in concepts like being in common, and so blithely ignored metaphysical principles, even that of non-contradiction.

The "intellectual" atmosphere of the time, which had come to reject Aristotle and Metaphysics, only confirmed him in this mental attitude. It will be seen that he did speak the language of the metaphysics of his scholastic teachers, but this he understood obviously as a kind of meta-physics that was simply more abstract than physics, something that mathematics could supply for.

However, without going more into this, we can straightaway detect the sloppiness of his reasoning. First of all, "is" comes before "is thinking" and "is" is contained in the proposition "I am thinking". So, he is not proving anything; he is merely pointing out something presupposed in what he says.

But, the more basic refutation of what he has done or tried to prove is that, in eliminating all intellectual principles or judgments prior to putting his own, he unwittingly includes the principle of non-contradiction, without which he cannot think (though like Heraclitus he may say) what he says.

For, take the first part of his "argument", "I think"; without adhering to the principle of non-contradiction, which says that "is" and "is not" are not the same, when he says "I am (is) thinking", he is prepared to allow that it can be the same as "I am not thinking". So, too, with the second part; "therefore I am" is no different in his mind from "therefore I am not". Thus, on his own presuppositions, he is no more saying "I think therefore I am" than "I do not think, therefore I am not". He is not really saying anything. One cannot think, that is make an intelligible judgment, unless one has first made the judgment in which the principle of non-contradiction is expressed.

Without applying the first principle of human thinking, Descartes' position is self-refuting. Yet, he believes he has discovered a marvellous means of escaping radical scepticism, and gathers a horde of other foolish followers, whose thinking incidentally does not rise above that of imagining. This is so much so that the English language begins to equate "I imagine" with "I conceive", and "unimaginable" with "inconceivable".

That should have been the end of Descartes's philosophical career. But there were all sorts of other influences at play at the beginning in the modern mind, not the least was Descartes's inventiveness as a mathematician, which contributed greatly to the progress of modern mathematical physics. Another was the humanist subjectivism that provided an intellectual alternative to a realist metaphysics, which had already been vehemently rejected because of its connection with Aristotle.

There were other moral causes that we have alluded to, but we will elaborate next upon the many influences that were in play prior to the emergence of the new "modern" age (the world soon to be thought of as a new world), all of which prepared the ground in a way for the Cartesian philosophy and science to play its part for the early modern world in overtaking the Aristotelian.

We have already, indeed from the start of this series of books, noted that the modern age was ushered in by a multitude of revolutions. These can be divided at the properly human level into radical changes in the life of knowledge or intellect and of appetite or will. As Catholics, we have to take into account that this life at the natural level was and is intertwined with life, knowledge and behaviour at the supernatural level, namely, as raised by grace, illumined by Faith and inspired by Charity. The refusal of grace, and loss of Faith, Hope and Charity has a devastating effect also on the natural order of human acts and habits.

As well, we have to see all human life, including social life since the time of Christ as ordered to governance by the Church, as the body of Christ embracing all mankind, but whose visible presence is subject to the limits of time and space and involves a process of evangelisation.

All this was realised in a manifest way throughout that period of time we know as Christendom. It seemed to some during that time that it was only a matter of time before the body of Christ, the Catholic Church, would spread uninterrupted over the whole known world. That was, however, a rather idealized view and in fact from its beginnings Christendom was marked by a series of set backs, from "forces" both internal and external.

Indeed, there was hardly a time when to many it seemed that the Christian civilization that the Church was the soul of was dying and would soon be dead. This prompted Chesterton, a good student of history as well as literature, to point to the only feature of the Church that could account for this, of having within it a principle of resurrection.

We mention only a couple of examples, though the most significant in the life of the Church, Arianism and Mohammedanism. As for the dire state in which Arianism put the Church, one has only to recall that in the very earliest stage of the Church St Jerome (259 AD) wrote, "the whole world groaned and marvelled to find itself Arian".

Externally, there was the overwhelming threat to Christianity by Mohammedanism. This had arisen to prominence in the eighth and succeeding centuries rapidly spreading to encroach upon the territories of Christian civilization so as to appear to be on the verge of overwhelming it. It was only at the battle of Lepanto (1571 AD) that its advance was halted. When we say external, we have to remember that this new religion has Judeo-

Christian origins and in fact adopts a similar position against the divinity of Christ as Arianism.

But merely by noting the date of 1571 it may be seen that if this threat was averted there had occurred much earlier in the same century another kind, if more internal nonetheless of such a revolutionary character as to threaten the very existence of Christianity as it had been known for over a thousand years, namely, what came to be called the Protestant Reformation.

The word "reform" belies the true character of the religious revolution involved. If initially those behind it were thinking in terms of reform, in the end they intended the destruction of the Catholic Church and meant in fact, coincident with other causes, the end of the era of Christendom. We are seeing in our own times the end result of this revolution, inevitably coming about much to the chagrin of the descendants of the original "reformers", many unable to understand how by casting off the Catholic Faith (of our fathers) we could not have retained the many natural goods of reason and science that seemed to be distinct from obedience to papal authority.

If they had held on to the wisdom of St. Thomas they would have been able to see that, as Pope Benedict XV said in his first general audience just after the commencement of the First World War, which we have quoted extensively in our previous book "Thomas of the Creator", the rejection of the Catholic Church and its divine authority, or Christian wisdom, must entail also the rejection of natural and practical wisdom, Metaphysics and

Ethics. It is no coincidence that at the same time the ancient wisdom best expressed by the pagan Aristotle was cast aside.

We might note incidentally the deviousness that one would have to expect in this process of rejection as it appears in the use of the word "reform", when it rather signifies "deform" or even destruction. It has been a pattern that has persisted in the thinking and practice of law and politics, begun in Protestant minded countries, to call the overturning of long held traditions of natural laws and institutions "law reform".

The most egregious and socially destructive may be seen in the history of "law reform" of the natural institution of marriage, culminating in the legalization of the grossest sexual sins in the redefinition of marriage to include "same sex marriage".

The notion that the parliament has the power to pass any law and call it a reform is now so entrenched that most lawyers think automatically in terms of positive law being able to override even the most fundamental of natural moral laws. Little do even Catholic lawyers (well indoctrinated in legal positivism) realise that they are being subtly sucked into supporting a regime more totalitarian than those they are at the same time being "educated" to be radically opposed to. They are virtually helpless to resist reforms even to legislate for murder of the most innocent and vulnerable, in the name of compassion and social utility.

However, though the deepest causes are supernatural, our focus is on the order of human nature, for the reasons given by Pope Benedict XVI in our previous book. Thus, we have paid attention to the many other revolutions that were occurring prior to "The Reformation" or soon following. The Cartesian revolution, which occurred soon after, is the one most evident in the order of intellect or science. But as we have noted, there were deeper moral causes.

The ethical order as we have seen exists and operates on three levels, personal, domestic and political. The personal is the most important and where moral life is nearest to the life of Faith. But we are focused on the social order, which includes the family and civil community. We have referred to the destruction of the domestic moral order, which is more fundamental than the civil or political. The evil at this familial level is obvious to a person of ordinary moral sense, yet modern society has become more and more desensitized to the destruction of the domestic moral order with the "progress" of the modern world.

There is an evil influence at the socio-political level, however, that is of major importance, not only because it rests in "the root of all evil", as St. Paul puts it, but also for reasons that we have tried to bring out, in modern times it has been able to conceal itself by the promotion of it in a politico-economic system, which for want of a better word we call Capitalism.

So, we have paid particular attention to a revolution that the modern mind wants not to be noticed. That is the revolution that was occurring before "The Reformation" and which the Reformers worked (consciously or unconsciously) to have it seen, when evident, as a good change in social behaviour, one of the prime benefits of freeing ourselves from the shackles of Catholic politico-economic morality.

This we may call the commercial and financial revolution coming to the fore towards the end of the era of Christendom. We have given extensive treatment to the revolution in money making and money lending that became an integral part of the new "economic reality". It is safe to say, as noted by Pope Benedict XV, that the love of money came to dominate the mentality and "morality" of the modern world that succeeded the old.

There were other revolutions, less hidden, that played important roles in giving the impression to modern man that the new era, a rejection of Catholicism, was greatly superior to the old, such as in science and technology, art and literature, political rule and individual freedom. Somehow or other, however, over time the promise of an era of earthly happiness from all these aspects of human "progress" seemed to slip further and further into the future, until eventually in recent times the mood of the brightest optimism has turned into that which the world experiences now of the darkest pessimism.

Here we want to focus on the intellectual revolution that is best seen in the work of Descartes. This is a revolution that the modern mind still is particularly proud of. But we have already pointed out its pernicious feature even from a philosophical and scientific point of view, a character that has worked its way into all modern philosophy and, in Hegel and Marx, came out in not only confirming the subjectivist basis of modern thought, but also in a kind of a bold proclamation of the power of contradiction within reality itself. The very use of the word "dialectic" is a clue to this move, for arguments "pro and con" are central to the exercise of this mental/rational art. Hegel simply fell for identifying the rational with the real.

This is not unrelated to something of the greatest importance in the analysis/criticism of Descartes's thinking. It is an error that so characterised his philosophy that it even put in the shade the most fundamental rejection of first intellectual judgments, this rejection coming obviously from his ignorance of Metaphysics and fixation on the clarity and distinction of his "ideas" verified in his imagination. The added error, however, was that what we know are not things outside, or being, but our own ideas. This is so patently false that even a child would laugh at the suggestion. Does anyone think that he is riding the idea of a horse? It is only some one locked into his imagination who would think he is dreaming as he fell off the horse.

It is obvious that his genial expertise in Mathematics, where one spends one's mental life in one's imagination (greatly enhanced in man by its "creative" ability), was a huge influence on Descartes's thinking, as it was on most of the intellectuals of the day (carrying through in modern thought even to Einstein). Though, as we shall note, Descartes continued to be interested in philosophy any real appreciation of the fundamental position of Metaphysics had been lost.

What we need to bring out is that this error was not original in Descartes. It appears to have been already connected with the change of focus onto the world around us, the natural order being newly discovered with the recovery of the empirical spirit we have discussed. In the case of Descartes it seems to be also associated with his education in philosophy by the late scholastics, particularly by the Jesuit influence from Suarez whose "Metaphysical Disputations" was thought to represent the scholastic inheritance, including Aquinas.

Unfortunately, as we have seen elsewhere, Suarez's philosophy, whilst mainly faithful in the moral and legal sphere, distorted St. Thomas's and Aristotle's Metaphysics. In short, we may put this down to his fallacious reading of the object/concept of being in a univocal way (influenced by Scotus). This is a fault that Aristotle warned of, to beware of the lack of power of the human intellect, so as to be led astray by the imperfect acts of the mind in their concepts (ratios) and proofs (argumentations). So easily do we slip in our notion of logic as analytic to dialectic, from science to opinion.

In the modern shift we have as well an application of analytic almost exclusively to the level of Mathematics. Thus, in regard to his "Rules for the Direction of the Mind", which he wrote late and did not complete, the Stanford University authority on him notes (1. 2): "In the Rules he sought to generalize the methods of mathematics so as to provide a route to clear knowledge of everything that human beings can know." This is the method that his admirers, such as Spinoza and Leibniz, took up and used to develop their own peculiar rationalist systems of philosophy.

In the order of Metaphysics, the fault can be related to the obsession with Logic that took over the late scholastic mind. Hence, we can say that Descartes inherited the subjectivism (in the special modern sense we have discussed), which was the basis of future idealism, not simply from the general anti-metaphysical (and anti-Aristotelian) temper of the new men of science, but specially from his scholastic (Jesuit) teachers in philosophy at La Fleche. It is what he evidently took for the metaphysics of Aristotle and Aquinas, and no doubt it was presented to him as such.

Descartes's mind then was divided between this "metaphysical" philosophizing and his intense concentration on what was a host of problems connected with the rise of the new physico-mathematics, which came to be regarded in Newton as the modern meaning of Science. As was the whole modern mind, Descartes was mesmerized by the amazing discoveries brought to light by the new empirico-mathematics, from which flowed even more amazing advances in technology. The conversion to the world was all but complete in the earliest time of the modern age.

The new association of empirical "research" with mathematics gave modern science an aura of magic that had long been connected with mathematics itself. We might note here Newton's fascination with alchemy. But initially it seems that it was the logico-mathematical side of Descartes philosophy that captured the minds of the new intellectuals, like Spinoza and Leibniz.

They were still much imbued with scholastic philosophy but in different ways. Spinoza took the lead of Geometry, and Monism, whilst Leibniz that of Arithmetic, and Pluralism. We do not wish to go into the details of their philosophies. We will say something more about Leibniz in our final two books because of his influence on modern logic and mathematics. We will only make a few comments here on Spinoza (1632-1677).

Being of Jewish heritage and education he would have been immersed in the Old Testament and the theology that had developed from the Talmud. But on contact with the modern mood, where the thought of Descartes had come to prominence in Holland, there were a number of other influences that he came under quite early in youth. We might note that on falling out with the Portugese Jewish hierarchy in Amsterdam, where he grew up, all these various influences came to the fore (Descartes remember had moved to live in Holland, possibly because of its reputation for liberalism).

Another interesting feature is that there Spinoza came in contact with an ex-Jesuit teacher who no doubt was up with the latest ideas. He already had a wide and diverse background in philosophy, ancient and mediaeval, such as the Stoics and Moses Maimonides. He was apparently acquainted with the leading lights of the day such as Machiavelli and Hobbes, whose political philosophies were based on power rather than justice. But, he obviously became most attracted to the new Cartesian notions and arguments and, without accepting Cartesian conclusions (as he stated himself), he developed a rationalist philosophy peculiarly his own.

The notion of God still dominated his thinking (hence his being called the God intoxicated philosopher) but he merged it with his notion of substance as the one absolute Being, reminiscent of Parmenides. Using the notion of modal difference, he then made Descartes's Thought and Extension simply two aspects of the one substance. But, possibly motivated by rebelliousness against religion, his plan was to write a major work on Ethics, as a justification of the absoluteness of individual freedom.

So it was that he became recognised as a champion of liberalism (and modern democracy) based on a view of religious authority of any kind as anti-freedom. All this, however, was to be proved by the use of the Cartesian method of theoretical proof (and made consistent with a quasi-pantheistic idea of God). This can be seen in the full title of his major work in Latin *Ethica More Geometrico Demonstrata.*

A major Catholic thinker influenced by Descartes was Malebranche. But we do not wish to pay much attention to thinkers such as these, whose particular ideas were not of such fundamental influence as that of Descartes's reinforcement of the internalized notion of subject, in effect substituting the human mind (Thought) for Aristotle's substance. This changed radically not only the notion of subject but also of object and so much has this entered into the thinking and language of modern man that it has been adopted at times by Catholic philosophers and theologians. One notable example is in an encyclical of Pope Saint John Paul II himself, namely, *Laborem exercens.* There he used "subjective" to refer to the worker as a human person as opposed to a mere object or thing. But this usage has become so deep seated that it is hardly possible to avoid it. One just has to be careful to make clear how it is used and avoid a false relativism that such a subjective language can foster.

This subjectivist/idealist feature of Descartes's philosophy came to dominate subsequent modern thinking and we will see it develop in Kant where the transcendental ego becomes the mysterious hidden cause of the known world in a way analogous to that of the unknown (and naturally unknowable) God as cause of being in traditional Metaphysics.

But before coming to Kant we need to say something about that school of modern philosophy that arose to oppose Cartesianism, without for that disputing its subjectivism. That is the school of British Empiricism, whose most famous members were the English John Locke, the Irish Bishop Berkeley and the Scot David Hume, the last being the most celebrated since.

Chapter 3

Descartes's philosophy captured the imagination (mind) not only of those who adopted his *a priori* mode of reasoning (though they might disagree with his conclusions), such as Spinoza and Leibniz, but also of those who objected to the use of this mode of reasoning as proceeding from ideas or principles naturally had in the mind – hence labeled "innate ideas".

Locke

Against this method of reasoning, deduction from abstract first principles, which is naturally adopted by a mathematician, John Locke argued that human knowledge did not originate in this way, but that all human knowledge originated in "experience". Thus was born the modern philosophy of Empiricism, which became the main opposition to the Cartesians, now labelled Rationalists.

However, though this opposition may appear to be relatively clear-cut, it is not so, and there are several distinctions that need to be brought out. First of all, we may note the apparent derivation of the empirical position from a well known Aristotelian dictum in Latin: *Omnis cognitio initium habet in sensu*, "every human knowledge has its beginning in sense"; put another way: "there is nothing in intellect that was not first in the senses".

This is a dictum that Descartes's necessarily denied. So he had to find the origin of his knowledge in his mind, which he automatically equated with his thinking faculty. We have noted the influence of the science and method of Mathematics on his thinking. We will note Locke's contrary acquaintance with the science and method of Natural Science or Physics. The dictum is most clearly shown in this order of sciences.

Descartes's use of *cogito* already points however to the confusion in his mind between the work of intellect and that of imagination, as we have explained. In fact, he went on to equate mental work, "thought" and "ideas", with all knowledge, of intellect or sense. Animals other than human or but machines, and even the human body is a machine.

Thus, he had already distorted the notion of knowledge as based in the having of forms of things other than the knower. This inevitably followed the cutting off of himself from the outside world and the objects of his senses.

It is to be carefully noted, however, that, though it appears that the empiricists are restoring "contact" with the outside world, they do not succeed in doing so, precisely because they have been sucked into the subjectivism of Descartes, and only make the distinction between thought and experience within the knowing subject, without reference to the outside world. We should note here the connection between this theoretical turn to focus on self and the more radical practical/moral turn that marked the religious revolution at the beginning of the modern era. It may seem coincidental, and here we are concerned with the theoretical turning inward, but both the practical and theoretical sides of the human spiritual soul involve the same turning away from reality and God.

The dispute between rationalism and empiricism comes to look like a dispute between intellectualists and sensists in regard to the content of human knowledge, but, because of Descartes's focus on the middle ground as it were of imagination, the two fields of knowledge are already confused in Descartes. The empiricists do but bring out more the dependence of human knowledge on the external senses, treating them, however, as if they were internal senses.

Thus, Locke and Co. use the same language of "ideas", but now reducing them to sense objects, whether simply taken, or as a construction into some sort of complex. It all gets rather muddled with Locke and the other empiricists proposing the discussion as one about the conditions of "human understanding", which phrase Aristotle and Aquinas reserve strictly to signify the activity of intellect. It goes without saying that the empiricists had no "idea" of the purely intellectual principle of non-contradiction, if they constantly used it verbally.

Locke was well educated, having gone to a prestigious school, Westminster in London, and then onto Oxford University. His family was not what one would call people of property, though his father was a lawyer who served in the army on the Puritan side during the civil war. But it was through the connections of his father's commander, who later went on to become a MP, that Locke was able to be afforded such a first class education.

On graduation at Oxford in those days one had to "take Anglican orders", with few exceptions of which Medicine was one. Locke elected to graduate in medicine. There he was able to acquire a good knowledge of natural science which no doubt fortified his empirical bent. His financial support was assured when Lord Anthony Ashleigh, later Earl of Shaftesbury, selected him as his personal physician.

At precisely the time that Locke was at Oxford "the new experimental philosophy had arrived", as the Stamford University article puts it. A group formed amongst those who were attracted to this new approach to the natural sciences, which was later to form the nucleus of the Royal Society. Locke became deeply involved in the discussions had frequently by this group focusing often on the experiments being undertaken. This was to have an important part to play in Locke's desire to find a basis for human knowledge.

It was through the later failure of the group to find an adequate "philosophical" explanation for our human knowledge that Locke turned his mind to study not the external source of our "understanding" but the internal conditions or limits on human knowledge. (Note how this turn lasted through to Kant). That was what led to his principal work of a theoretical nature "An Essay Concerning Human Understanding." In this he laid out his thesis, opposing that of Descartes, that the exclusive source of all knowledge from the lowest to the highest was "experience", which he basically held as mere sense experience, but not without some sophistication.

For, it is to be remembered that, though he reacted with the mood of the times against it, he had had a thorough education in scholastic philosophy, and had to take into account some evident problems that remained. There are a couple of adjustments made by him that we will mention here. The first was to do with adding "reflective" knowledge to experience and the other was the distinction he made between primary and secondary qualities in regard to the reality of sense objects.

As best as we can make out, for Locke "reflection" was a part of our sense knowledge and would seem to be an attempt to distinguish the intuitive knowledge of sensible things had by our external senses and the equally intuitive knowledge had by our sense consciousness.

Scholasticism accounted for the latter by a separate faculty called the common or unitive sense, by which the animal was distinctly aware not just of the things sensed but also of its very sensations (cf. our "Psychology Science and Saint Thomas Aquinas"). What they called consciousness, or co-knowledge, Locke called reflection. Properly understood, which is impossible to empiricists, it is a valid distinction and reflective is not a bad way to describe it.

It seems that Locke did not really appreciate that it was the product of a separate sense faculty and, because of his reduction of ideas from being intellectual and abstract to images and sense impressions, had to confuse sense consciousness with intellective consciousness. The latter is naturally self-reflective and does not need a separate faculty to explain it. Within the one object of one's intellect (reason) are both the thing known and one's knowing of it. That would be a reason why modern philosophers have a tendency to identify even direct knowledge as such with consciousness.

The other "adjustment" made by Locke was between primary and secondary qualities, the latter inconsistently treated here as only within the knower. It no doubt came from the distinction the scholastics made (based in Aristotle) between proper and common sensibles, the former being the objects of the external senses, like colour to sight, and the latter being listed as size, shape, number, motion and rest, came to be regarded differently in relation to external material things.

But this difference had already been affected by the major role mathematics had come to play in the new physico-mathematics, already being developed by both Descartes and Galileo. We have already seen the turn in late scholasticism to subjectivism. The germ of idealism was in the late scholastics but, with the admiration for the real usefulness of mathematical science, there was a sort of half way house position adopted.

This we can see in Galileo in his belief that nature, as the physical world, was "written" by God in the language of Mathematics. Thus, Galileo also apparently held the distinction used by Locke. It may be noticed that the common sensibles (called common because able to be sensed by more than one sense) have or can be given a quantitative character. Galileo regarded these objects as reality based, but colour etc., not so. This disconnected the sensible qualities from their proper objects in the physical world and so was the beginning of the placing of the objects of our knowledge wholly within our own nature, unrelated to anything outside, which is what "subjective" came to mean.

This internalization of the world in the "subject" as mind that was complete and clear cut in Descartes was not so with Locke, for he was affected still by concepts hanging over from scholasticism, such as the notion of substance. A horse is not just a certain sized shape impinging on our vision or touch. Though demanded by intellect, a notion of substance (also for Aristotle a subject) was beyond our sense experience. For, sense knowledge was limited to appearances of things through their accidental features. In any case the idealist presupposition made anything outside the knowing subject unintelligible.

All that Locke could do was say that substance existed, but was "I know not what" (a position later taken by Kant in his use of the word "noumenon").The absurdity of modern philosophical positions is clear from the rejection of Metaphysics and the principle of non-contradiction. Contradictions in what the modern philosophers say all over the place, but they are blithely passed over, and are generally regarded as not all that "critical".

But, it is possible to say some particular truths if one forgets for the moment this deliberate denial. This is the position of those moderns engaged in the particular sciences of Mathematics, Physics and Physico-mathematics. It is only when the modern mind is pushed to the limits to justify the truth of these sciences that the absurdity of their basic positions comes out. Then it is a matter, however, of burying one's head in the sand, or trying to talk under water. The succession of ideologies that results is as evanescent and ephemeral as the bubbles that rise to the surface in the second exercise. "What's the latest?"

The empiricists do not avoid the radical skepticism that attaches to their philosophy of science (as neither did Descartes). They just imagine that they are avoiding the dogmatism that seems to belong to Cartesianism, which also is believed to be a feature of Aristotelianism (and Thomism).

Hence, they are comfortable with treating first principles as hypotheses (a violation of the second condition of the principle of non-contradiction). Karl Popper expressed this as the "principle" that unless some theory of science could be falsified it was not truly scientific. But this merely denotes a confusion of the conditions of principles of Metaphysics (and Mathematics) with those of Physics or the natural sciences (Natural Philosophy).

Aristotle had already explained that the laws of Natural Science held not absolutely but "for the most part". This is because there is necessarily "sensible matter" in the object. Thus, an animal is naturally born with one head. If, as may occur, an animal body is found to be born with two heads, that exception does not invalidate the rule, it proves it on account of its rarity. Yet this possibility led an empiricist or positivist like J. S. Mill (Bertrand Russell's godfather) to say that the laws of mathematics, such that 2+2=4, are not certain but only have a (high) degree of probability.

This illustrates what Aristotle has said about the sources of doubts about the principle of non-contradiction. They are either from deficiency in our intellectual power, or in the condition of the object. The first gives rise to disputes among thinkers with the opinion of one contradicting another. This is the area of the mind where logic is equated with dialectic (and sophistic). The classical figure here mentioned by Aristotle is Protagoras. The second sources is where scientists and philosophers focus too much on the changing nature of material things, as was the case with the early natural philosophers and is almost the sole preoccupation of modern thought.

The difference between the ancient and modern tendency to radical skepticism is the dominance of Mathematics in the notion of Physics. The classical ancient figure here, however, was Heraclitus (also referred to by Aristotle), who was so misled by the changeable condition of material things, i.e. nature as physical, that he openly denied the metaphysical principle of non-contradiction. The modern theory of materialist evolution plays the same role for the modern mind. It is noteworthy how it is used by both Hegel and Marx.

Locke early belonged to the second class of modern empiricist-based skeptics, the mixed nature of whose anti-metaphysical (and anti-Aristotelian) thought was purified by David Hume, as we shall see. But, as is common with many modern "speculative" thinkers, Locke became deeply involved in the practical politics of the time (Shaftesbury being a leading political figure embroiled in the events leading up to the "Glorious Revolution" of 1689).

Locke's writings on practical principles in politics and morality became as deeply influential in modern behavior as his thought was in the philosophy of science. His influence on the American struggle for independence from Britain is well known and documented. We do not wish to go into this side of his philosophy here, as we are concerned only with the "speculative" order of thinking.

Our previous books deal with these practical subjects. But we mean to deal more fully with the modern deviations not only in theoretical science but also in practical science in our final book where we will have more to say on Locke, as he is such a pivotal figure.

We will only note here that the thought of Locke and the others belonging to the empiricist and positivist "tradition" (though not always clearly distinguished from the rationalist and idealist strains of modern thought) can be traced back to the religious and other revolutions that occurred around the beginning of the modern era, with the most fundamental the rejection of the divine authority of the Catholic Church, and most sinisterly to original sin and human pride.

We are concerned here to relate it to the rejection of Metaphysics and Ethics. With regard to Politics (and Economics) we can see the influence of early figures, such as Machiavelli and Francis Bacon (whose mixing of theoretical science and practical politics Locke curiously mirrors). Francis Bacon was an admired of Machiavelli's switching of the focus of politics from morality/justice to power/realpolitik. This turn to power politics has a connection with the politico-economic theory of Capitalism. But we will deal more fully with this radical change in the understanding of the nature and end of government later.

There is one other feature of Locke's philosophy that we should bring out and that is his treatment of the place of abstraction in the formation of what he regarded as more complex ideas. But since this is the central focus of Bishop Berkeley's peculiar place in the line of the British school of empiricism, we will deal with it in discussing Berkeley next.

Berkeley

The inclusion of Berkeley, an Anglo-Irish bishop, in the British empiricist school (and one admired at that) is its most curious feature. For the position of its first proponent, Locke, was decidedly non-religious, if not anti-religious (as with all religious sentiment of the time, he was decidedly anti-Catholic) and at its end in Hume its atheism came clearly out.

What is more, Berkeley saw the Lockean reading of experience as somehow derived from a material outside world, and therefore rooted in materialism. What this meant we will look at closer below. But Berkeley viewed what he regarded as materialism as so pernicious that he worked to eliminate the notion of material body altogether. In opposition to the existence of "matter", which Locke was prepared to allow (even as existing in a stone) is not inconsistent with thinking. Berkeley posited that the only reality was purely spiritual (stones as well presumably). He declared openly that the overall motive of his critiques was religious. But here again we have to examine more closely Berkeley's notion of spirit.

Though most would find his "immaterialism" simply a too extreme spiritualist version of our world, there is reluctance, for reasons perhaps clear from what we have said above, to use the words "false" or "absurd" of his philosophy. The modern dodge is to call it "counter-intuitive". What intrigues many is how sharp and accurate are his criticisms of the major intellectual figures of his time, such as Descartes, Locke, and even Newton, able to match them at both the philosophical and scientific levels.

So it is that he is still regarded as a major modern philosopher and especially in the context of modern science. Even today, in the latest entry in the prestigious Stanford University Encyclopedia of Philosophy, he is described as "one of the great philosophers of the early modern period". It is the theoretical aspect of his thought, however, that we are concerned with in this book. We do not consider his practical/moral philosophy.

Berkeley was born in 1685 at his family home, Dysart Castle, County Kilkenny, Ireland, the eldest son of William Berkeley of the noble family of Berkeley who had served as feudal lords and landowners in England. He was educated at Kilkenny College and attended Trinity College Dublin, even then apparently having the status of a University, but because of the requirement of taking an Anglican oath, exclusive of non-Anglicans at the time and much afterwards (the original Catholic university in Ireland was dissolved following the Reformation).

He was elected a Scholar in 1702, being awarded BA in 1704 and MA and a Fellowship in 1707. He later taught Greek at Trinity College. So it can be seen that he was well educated and of some means. He became a cleric in the Church of Ireland, which was the name for the Church of England in Ireland at that time still under English rule. He lived for 68 years and for the last 20 or so years was bishop of Cloyne.

Kilkenny College was a prestigious school which has had many famous students including Jonathan Swift, the author of Gulliver's Travels, who was at the college at much the same time as Berkeley. Swift also became a cleric and hence was generally known as Dean Swift. Students of the college could go on to Trinity College Dublin, as did Berkeley at a very early age.

It is most important to understand the intellectual climate at the time and particularly in the universities. If at the time Locke was at Oxford well before Berkeley was born that "the new experimental philosophy had arrived", things had "progressed" rapidly in the move away from scholasticism (as thought to be derived from Aristotle's philosophy and science, associated with contempt for ancient and medieval natural science for reasons we have dealt with). It was no coincidence that this intellectual "reformation" was also associated with a protestant belief that Catholics could not be persons of independent mind because of their "blind faith" and servile acceptance of papal authority. The motif of "freedom" of will in the individual person was strongly in play.

So it was that at Trinity the curriculum that the young Berkeley encountered was "notably modern" and, despite his religious leanings, it seems that practically his whole focus was on the exciting new physical science and the related philosophical theories of Descartes, Locke and others. As one Internet source puts it, "Berkeley encountered the new science and philosophy of the late seventeenth century, which was characterized by hostility towards Aristotelianism." It goes on to say: "Berkeley's works display his keen interest in natural philosophy [...] from his earliest writings (*Arithmetica*, 1707) to his latest (*Siris*, 1744). Moreover, much of his philosophy is shaped fundamentally by his engagement with the science of his time." The profundity of this interest can be judged from numerous entries in Berkeley's *Philosophical Commentaries* (1707–1708), e.g. "Mem. to Examine & accurately discuss the scholium of the 8th Definition of Mr Newton's Principia." (#316)

Berkeley, as noted, criticised many of the leading lights of the new science, including Newton. His critique of Locke's distinction between primary and secondary qualities, to which we have referred, is of special significance not only to his adoption of a general and most radical form of idealism but also to the later rejection of Newtonian absolutism by the "New Physics" of the early twentieth century, as we shall see.

Locke had argued that "secondary qualities", such as colour and heat, are not objective in the sense of being in the material things or bodies that we regard as what we perceive (see or feel). He took the familiar example of immersing each of one's hands into water, one containing hot water and the other cold water. Then on removing both hands and placing them into a third container of water one experiences different degrees of heat in the different hands. He concluded that there cannot be heat in the water that is felt. Somehow or other, the "idea" of heat must come from within the sense of touch. That conclusion may be generalized for all such secondary qualities.

Locke, however, maintained, along with Galileo, that the primary qualities, which we have described, could be regarded as in the thing. Berkeley's first major work (An Essay Towards a New Theory of Vision) aimed to refute Locke's position and argued that this relativity applied in the case of all objects of sight, whether secondary as colour or primary as shape, size and so on. From this he concluded that all objects of our experience had to be our own "ideas". How this is connected with his notion of spirits we will come to shortly. It may be seen, however, how this does not dispute the general idealist position that underlay modern thought. Berkeley's reasoning only worked to confirm and universalise it.

One thing to note here regarding the traditional scholastic position, however, is that a distinction was made between what were called the higher external senses, such as sight and hearing, and the lower, such as touch, taste and smell. A certain relativity or "subjective" element was allowed in the case of the lower, as would explain the case of the feeling of heat. But, generally speaking, the objects of the higher external senses, especially of sight, were thought to be purely "objective", i.e. in things as they are outside our sensing.

This had particular application to the understanding of the illumination of light, say from the sun, as being instantaneous (contrary to the modern notion of the speed of light). In principle though, it is to be understood that the relativity comes from the fact that, besides being an organ of external sense, the organ itself is a body and as such subject to the same changes in "qualities" as bodies generally.

It is to be expected, therefore, that there will be in all organic faculties of knowledge, i.e. senses, a degree of natural bodily affection or change in one way or another (if in some cases too minimal for any relativity to be discerned). The older mistakes can be explained as owing to lack of sufficient ability to discern miniscule changes in regard to our perception of the object. So, absoluteness was assumed in the assessment of the objects of sight. Nonetheless, in obvious cases the relativity in the judgment was known, as in the case of motion where one is moving at the same or at a different rate (or at rest) to the thing observed in motion.

Berkeley's point against Locke is therefore well taken. But, where he errs is in interpreting this as emptying any reality from the qualities in and actions of the external thing. (This is to be taken formally and not reduced as Locke did to a notion of efficient causality). That is to say, he mistakes the real relativity for the absolute non-existence of the form had in the thing and concludes the form known must exist only in the knower. Even an elementary reading of Aristotle would have given an understanding of knowledge as the having of the form of another thing besides one's own natural form or forms. The modern philosophers of knowledge had the disadvantage of not understanding the very nature of knowledge.

Berkeley's success in his argument against Locke only served to reinforce the idealist philosophy that had already been transmitted into modern thought through the likes of Descartes. However, it is this pointing up of relativity in physical and physico-mathematical science that his work came later to be seen as presaging the necessary correction of the absolutism that was basic feature of Newton's physics (mathematical physics).

The work of Berkeley therefore was useful in the advance of modern science, but not because of its promotion of philosophical Idealism, even though major figures in that movement claimed him. It is remarked of German philosopher Arthur Schopenhauer that he wrote of him: "Berkeley was, therefore, the first to treat the subjective starting-point really seriously and to demonstrate irrefutably its absolute necessity. He is the father of idealism ...".

Relativity, however, is not opposed to realism. Furthermore, it is only to be taken into account in sense knowledge and therefore in natural science (including mathematical physics), where the objects, and the subjects, are not entirely free from matter. The moderns, ignorant of Metaphysics, cannot fail to avoid the sources of error that Aristotle warned of so long ago.

Aristotle put one of the two sources of error in Metaphysics as what amounts to an exclusive focus on natural science (and Mathematics – another spider trap for the precocious young mind). It is noteworthy of the empiricists that their minds were formed in their youth and they spent the rest of their lives defending their immature theories. This is particularly noticeable in the case of David Hume, which we will find when we come to him.

The other source of error is from the weakness of the human intellect, which is uncomfortable in Metaphysics and falls back into a dialectical mode, arguing about the opinions of others. The human mind then is particularly focused on practical moral affairs and politics. Another thing to notice about these early modern "philosophers" is their habit of latching on to political patrons and becoming their advisers, thus becoming experts in political science or philosophy. But, in this book we are not concerned here with this practical side of their thought. We will hopefully bring all together in our last book in this series (12th).

It is bad enough when the very distinction of knowledge from other vital life and activity is lost. Even within the confused notion of human knowledge the words "thought" and "idea" are used to cover all human knowledge from the lowest sense impressions to the highest intellectual ones. Descartes has already made this confusion simply by equating thought with everything internal to human life and activity, not just to information or inclinations. The empiricists carried this on with a vengeance, in the process reducing all internal knowledge and inclination to the sense level.

Not having the benefit of distinctions forged by intellectual geniuses over centuries, they succeeded only in making an awful mess even of the distinction between intellect and sense. They spoke the language of understanding but applied it to the animal side of human knowledge. What we need to restore is an elementary understanding of understanding itself. Wish us luck.

The thing that is completely missed by the modern mind is the twofold source of human intellectual knowledge. They are external things and an internal light (which the scholastics called rather obscurely the agent intellect). The best comparison is in showing that the act of sight depends upon two sources (both external),colour and light. Colour is a quality of bodies, something in bodily or material things without which one cannot see (or see only peripherally). But without light the colour is not visible. So the object of sight is illuminated colour, with colour fully actual able to be understood as a sort of incorporated light. Such a materialization of the form of light proportions the object to our animal eyesight. We can in a way see light but it is rather a case of not being able to see without light.

So, too, in an analogous way is it with the human intellect that has the act of understanding or intellection (called potential or receiving to distinguish it from the agent intellect/light of understanding). The essences or natures of things are to it like the forms of colour are to the power and act of sight. They have to be proportioned to the human intellect by the abstractive function of the agent intellect (not essentially different from illuminating/actuating function).

But we can see that without the forms or essences had from things (such as the nature of horse) there can be no understanding. Neither is it possible to understand these essences without their illumination by the light of understanding. These are two necessary sources of human intellectual knowledge.

In this regard we can identify two opposed intellectual errors, which can be traced back to denying or ignoring one or other of these sources. The idealist is on the side of those who reject the things (in their essences or natures); and propose that what we know are only our own ideas. The materialist/realist (insofar as he rejects the need for any internal intellectual/spiritual light) proposes that our human knowledge can be explained solely in terms of the influence of the external things' activity on our bodies. This position is commonly called materialist, equating material things with all reality.

This, however, brings in all sorts of confusions, the most relevant one here to do with the notion of spirit. Since Descartes, the modern mind has almost invariably equated thought and ideas with what is internal as opposed to things external, with Descartes going to the extreme of opposing the internal and external in terms of activity and passivity, using the geometrical form of extension as equated with body, even our own bodies.

Thus goes out the window all the fine distinctions between bodily activity from non-living nature, like fire, to living nature, like a tree, to animal nature, like a horse, and as we note even the human body, all of which Descartes treated as machines moved by something of spiritual soul, like a boy riding a bike. How anyone could stomach this mess we find hard to comprehend. But his works are the first studied in modern faculties of philosophy!

Berkeley reacted against this materialism (virtually reduced to the concept of primary matter – with which Locke got the concept of substance confused)but his (Berkeley's) notion of spirit was equally obscure. For, he seems to have simply taken over from Descartes that anything internal to human nature, focusing on knowledge virtually identified with ideas, was spiritual. Yet this caused a problem with providing for spirits. As generally noted in articles on him, "According to Berkeley there are only two kinds of things: spirits and ideas. Spirits are simple, active beings which produce and perceive ideas; ideas are passive beings which are produced and perceived".

His position in this regard is often summarized in the curt Latin phrase *esse est percipi*, which means to be is to be perceived. But that would limit reality to ideas and leave no room for what must have the ideas, which had to be taken as "mind", and which Berkeley took to be a spirit. To make any sense then the full phrase has to be *esse est percipi (aut percipere)*—to be is to be perceived (or to perceive). Yet that still poses a problem for Berkeley. If only what is known are our ideas, and we can only know spirits as the causes of ideas, we have no idea of spirits any more than we have of God.

Because of the looseness in the definition of the terms used, there are all sorts of problems with such a principle so far as assuming that the perceiver is spiritual. For dogs have sense perceptions. Otherwise they would not chase cats. So in terms of Berkeley's own concepts the cats chased by dogs exist only in the perceptions (ideas) of the dogs.

It may be noticed here that the two sources of human understanding reduce to one when we understand that God is the cause of both things and the light of our understanding. St. Thomas refined St. Augustine's position here. Whereas St. Augustine posed God as the light of our understanding St. Thomas said that though that is true it does not exclude the fact that God has given man his own light of understanding whereby he understands and that our light of understanding is a participation in the divine light.

It is God as the cause of things that is also the cause of our understanding through the things he has made. Berkeley took as a proof for the existence of God the existence of spirit. But in cutting us off from external material things we lose an essential source of any knowledge that we have and without it the internal source is inoperative. So it is that in denying the existence of material things, or the certainty of our knowledge of them, we cannot come to know the existence of God, as their necessary cause.

So Berkeley's fundamental error is the same as all modern thinkers in so far as they maintain that what we first know are our own ideas. It is just that most are not as clear thinking as he is and take positions focused on the material world whilst ignoring the metaphysical principles upon which the particular sciences are based.

These sciences can be practised and with success with the metaphysical principles held implicitly. So, it is only when the "philosophers of science" face the question of the foundations that they indulge in all sorts of nonsense. As we have seen, relativity is mistaken for proof of unreality on the part of the things investigated. Then some are persuaded that there is justification for a basically sceptical attitude towards conclusions that are firmly established.

We can bring out how Berkeley's idealist philosophy has been used by recent philosophers of science by quoting from an Internet entry on Karl Popper. It is meant only to show how convoluted the discussion can become. But following this we will say something about how Berkeley's bringing out of relativity in sense or empirical knowledge is useful to understanding the change in modern physics (mathematical physics) from the absolutism in Isaac Newton to relativism in Albert Einstein. We do not go into the significance of the other change in modern science from determinism to indeterminism. That will have to be dealt with elsewhere.

"Berkeley's razor is a rule of reasoning proposed by the philosopher Karl Popper in his study of Berkeley's key scientific work *De Motu*. Berkeley's razor is considered by Popper to be similar to Ockham's razor but 'more powerful'. It represents an extreme, empiricist view of scientific observation that states that the scientific method provides us with no true insight into the nature of the world. Rather, the scientific method gives us a variety of partial explanations about regularities that hold in the world and that are gained through experiment. The nature of the world, according to Berkeley, is only approached through proper metaphysical speculation and reasoning. Popper summarises Berkeley's razor as such:

A general practical result—which I propose to call 'Berkeley's razor'—of [Berkeley's] analysis of physics allows us *a priori* to eliminate from physical science all essentialist explanations. If they have a mathematical and predictive content they may be admitted *qua* mathematical hypotheses (while their essentialist interpretation is eliminated). If not they may be ruled out altogether. This razor is sharper than Ockham's: *all* entities are ruled out except those which are perceived.

In another essay of the same book titled "Three Views Concerning Human Knowledge", Popper argues that Berkeley is to be considered as an instrumentalist philosopher, along with Robert Bellarmine, Pierre Duhem and Ernst Mach. According to this approach, scientific theories have the status of serviceable fictions, useful inventions aimed at explaining facts, and without any pretension to being true. Popper contrasts instrumentalism with the above-mentioned essentialism and his own "critical rationalism".

There is much to chew over here. We have a hint of what St. Thomas called "saving the appearances", which is how he viewed the Ptolemaic Astronomy. The use of the word instrumentalism is confusing in this context and can be misleading. Logic is an instrument of science, but that does not rule out the reality of the concepts used or the certainty of the conclusions. The term here is used rather to refer to what Aristotle called logical beings or *entia rationis*, which are fictional in a sense of purely logical tools but not for that opposed to having a science of truth. Popper gets into quite a muddle here, opposing the words "instrumentalist" and "essentialist". There are many distinctions that can only be brought out properly by a thorough study of St. Thomas's use of the word "reason" and how it is variously applied in the case of different sciences.

But let us move on to how Berkeley is viewed as anticipating the relativism that adjusted the absolutist assumptions of Newtonian Physics (mathematical), which culminated in Einstein's theory of general relativity. Unfortunately, when one extreme is avoided the tendency is for the "corrections" to be taken to the other extreme. This seems to have occurred with the new physics (mathematical physics) though we do not want to go into the labyrinth of details that the discussion of modern physicists has been engaged on.

As Berkeley did himself, the relativity discovered is mistaken as evidence of subjectivity in the ideal sense, with the correlative error of taking science as failing to reach the real world outside at all so that the scientist must be content with "mathematical hypotheses", as Popper contends. All "essentialist explanations" must be eliminated. Apart from making all science science-fiction, this means that there is no science of being, and is a blatant rejection of the principle of non-contradiction. It also confirms the idealistic presupposition that underlies all modern thought.

Like Popper, most if not all modern philosophers of science, and indeed of knowledge itself, take a partial insight into the role of reason in "saving the appearances", which can be useful, but so universalize it as to make it not just an error in Physics but also in Metaphysics. Not to be too cynical it provides a mental world in which adolescent minds (including professors) spend most of their academic time producing papers for peer review that are then consigned to the never to be read again section of the university library's data bank. The only time they are taken out of the "bank" is to include them in one's CV as a long list of peer review articles.

It is clear that in the case of Berkeley the relativity was taken to the extreme of Idealism. In the case of Einstein it seems that he allowed it to invade the field of Mathematics (Geometry) when its application strictly belongs to natural science because Mathematics so abstracts from matter as to exclude sensible motion or change. So it is that it is as if we are children at a magic show, hypnotized by all sorts of absurdities (geometrically straight lines bending and time going backwards) that seem to follow the discoveries of the new physics.

Berkeley and his philosophy have had a strange influence on modern thinking and education, even generally, especially in the USA. Besides having a city and university named after him, the circumstances of which we will come to shortly, he seemed to exercise a fascination on the modern mind, no doubt because of the strength of the idealist element in it, despite its being "counter-intuitive" to the otherwise deep materialist influence.

Below is a recount of his reception on his visit to America. "When Berkeley visited America, the American educator Samuel Johnson [not the English Dr. Samuel Johnson, who famously refuted Berkeley's view that nothing is material by kicking a rock. 'Thus I refute him!' he reportedly declared] paid Berkeley a visit." The story goes on "the two later corresponded. Johnson convinced Berkeley to establish a scholarship program at Yale, and to donate a large number of books as well as his plantation to the college when the philosopher returned to England. It was one of Yale's largest and most important donations; it doubled its library holdings, improved the college's financial position and brought Anglican religious ideas and English culture into New England. Johnson also took Berkeley's philosophy and used parts of it as a framework for his own American Practical Idealism school of philosophy. As Johnson's philosophy was taught to about half the graduates of American colleges between 1743 and 1776, and over half of the contributors to the *Declaration of Independence* were connected to it, Berkeley's ideas were indirectly a foundation of the American Mind."

From this we can understand how extensive and deep-seated Berkeley's influence is in not just the American but also the whole world education system. With Harvard, Yale and Berkeley Universities are "officially" regarded as the three most prestigious in the world. Melbourne and Sydney, however, manage to get into the top 40.

The story of the founding of the city of Berkeley and the university of the same name located within it is equally intriguing.

The details can be readily gathered from the Internet but we put below a short account that gives one as good an idea as any. It should be noted that Berkeley thought European civilization was in decline and put his hopes in the New World. Such was his reason for spending time in America.

Both the University of California, Berkeley and the city of Berkeley California, were named after him, although the pronunciation has evolved to suit American English: (/ˈbɜːrkli/ *BURK-lee*). The naming was suggested in 1866 by Frederick H. Billings, a trustee of the then College of California. Billings was inspired by Berkeley's *Verses on the Prospect of Planting Arts and Learning in America*, particularly the final stanza: "Westward the course of empire takes its way; the first four Acts already past, a fifth shall close the Drama with the day; time's noblest offspring is the last".

The following are just other minor instances of the influence of Berkeley. That will close our treatment of him here.

The Town of Berkeley, currently the least populated town in Bristol County, Massachusetts, was founded on 18 April 1735 and named after the renowned philosopher. It is located 40 miles south of Boston and 25 miles north of Middletown, Rhode Island.

A residential college and an Episcopal seminary at Yale University also bear Berkeley's name.

Berkeley Preparatory School in Tampa, Florida, a private school affiliated with the Episcopal Church, is also named for him.

Bishop Berkeley's Gold Medals" are two awards given annually at Trinity College Dublin, "provided outstanding merit is shown", to candidates answering a special examination in Greek. The awards were founded in 1752 by Berkeley.

An Ulster History Circle blue plaque commemorating him is located in Bishop Street Within, city of Derry.

Berkeley's farmhouse in Middletown, Rhode Island, is preserved as Whitehall Museum House, also known as Berkeley House, and was listed on the National Register of Historical Places in 1970. St. Columba's Chapel, located in the same town, was formerly named "The Berkeley Memorial Chapel," and the appellation still survives at the end of the formal name of the parish, "St. Columba's, the Berkeley Memorial Chapel".

We move now to consider the last and most influential of the three British empiricists, David Hume.

Hume

Hume's project is not unlike that of Descartes. That is, he looked at the scene of the philosophical discussions of his time and saw nothing but a multitude of conflicting opinions. "There is nothing which is not the subject of debate, and in which men of learning are not of contrary opinions." (Introduction) Hume then thought to devise his own system of thought, inspired by the success of Newton's "experimental method" in his new Physics. Newton's he took as a science of nature as physical (Hume hardly distinguished the mathematical part).

The philosophical problems with which Hume was concerned were in regard to the most general and fundamental of questions. These he sometimes called "metaphysical" but the term he initially used was "moral". By this he did not mean what is normally meant by moral philosophy or ethical science but what he called the philosophy of Man, or the science of human nature. This included and indeed was first focused on what Aristotle and Aquinas called human psychology.

So it was that the first part of his treatise was on this aspect of human nature (covering human understanding and the passions, both of which notions require careful attention to what Hume meant by them - by no means consistent with the traditional Aristotelian meanings). After this came the study of "Morals" taken more strictly.

But what it is important to notice right from the start is that Hume considered the study of human nature as the most fundamental of all sciences. "It is evident, that all the sciences have a relation, greater or less, to human nature: and that however wide any of them may seem to run from it, they still return back by one passage or another. Even Mathematics, Natural Philosophy, and Natural Religion, are in some measure dependent on the science of MAN; since they lie under the cognizance of men, and are judged of by their powers and faculties." He elaborates on this: "And as the science of man is the only solid foundation for the other sciences, so the only solid foundation we can give to this science itself must be laid on experience and observation."

To this we may relate Aristotle's comment that if man (or "Humanity") were the highest thing then Politics, not Metaphysics, would be the most fundamental science. That in fact is how things turned out for Hume and all modern thinking, as we shall see.

Therein lay Hume's first mistake, that throws himself back upon himself from considering the world of being that is the true object of Metaphysics, and where he could appreciate the certainty of the first metaphysical principles, the very first of which is the principle of non-contradiction. This is undermined at the start as it was in Descartes when the focus turns inward to oneself, in the name here of Man. We can see how it may have the practical/moral aspect of pride.

In theoretical terms this turn inwards caused the late scholastics to construct the idealistic presupposition we have discussed. Hume does not explicitly address the fact that in focusing on sense impressions he is falling into this subjectivist condition of mind, but it was there in his predecessors Locke and Berkeley. When he comes to consider whence these impressions might come Hume simply dodges the question as insoluble.

But it does not matter so far as the destruction of the intelligibility of the real world is concerned. For the very limiting of human knowledge to sense that Hume effects reduces man to the level of an animal without understanding. In Book I there is in fact a section headed 'OF THE REASON OF ANIMALS'(Section XVI Part III), which states: "no truth appears to me more evident, than that beasts are endowed with thought and reason as well as men." We may note at this point that Hume had a rather crass notion of the higher capabilities of animals. He did not really know how to distinguish an animal's natural judgment or instinct from human judgment and prudence.

This misuse of the notion of reason would be enough on its own to convict Hume of eliminating a spiritually based intelligibility and rationality from the knowledge belonging to human nature. The use of reason on such irrational premises can only lead to radical scepticism, the very result Hume wanted to overcome. Once one has seen the reduction of human knowledge to the level of the brute animal there is really no need to proceed. But we will go through the fundamental concepts and propositions from which Hume built up his philosophy. Before this, however, we will make some further preliminary points.

The difference between Descartes's and Hume's projects was that Descartes thought he had found the true and certain philosophy or science of reality (using his expertise in the mathematical method of reasoning). Hume initially too felt he had found the true scientific method in Newton's experimental side of his physico-mathematics. We can say that it was the certainty induced in the human mind by the mathematical side of Newton's science that gave Hume his initial confidence but he ended up employing the experimental method in such a thoroughly sensist way that it destroyed all confidence in certainty and in fact undermined all science (Kant's project was to try to rescue Newtonian science from this result).

Thus, in trying to escape from the prevailing skepticism (generated by the interminable disputations referred to) Hume ended up in a skepticism just as radical as the ones he wished to avoid, if he did not quite see it that way. His only escape from this paradoxical result of the use of reason (human understanding), as he saw it, was to exit "the philosophical club" and return "to the street", where one lives by "custom" rather than reason.

The clubbish cliques today are rather among university academics, but in Hume's time they extended to the congenial literary and artistic world, best represented in the salons of the French well to do. There is much in common between Hume and Voltaire in this regard. In a way, we might just note here that this quasi-coffee shop style of discussing the burning issues of the day has returned with the social networks of the Internet, but at a much lower level of intelligence, quite obviously.

It may be noted that neither Hume nor Voltaire ever held an academic post, yet came to rule the world of the philosophy of the time. Hume was rather contemptuous of "professors", believing he could learn more by his own studies than from teachers such as those he encountered at Edinburgh University. Such was the impact of Newton's scientific revolution, however, it was regarded as much the property of the world as of the learned. It was not as if Hume did not seek later in life an academic post (possibly for financial reasons) but by then his reputation for atheism excluded him.

There is also a coincidence in the experience had of Newton and Locke by both Voltaire and Hume. Voltaire spent some time in England where he became thoroughly familiar with Newtonian science and Lockean philosophy. Hume, already familiar with Newton and Locke (and Berkeley) spent some time in France, where he no doubt came in contact with the leaders of the French Enlightenment. In fact he stayed at La Fleche where there were still Jesuits teaching at the school attended by Descartes. It is said that Hume enjoyed "baiting" the Jesuits who were there.

There was great excitement engendered by the Newtonian physico-mathematical science and its apparent replacement of the "old" natural science. Coincidentally, there would also have been a strong feeling of release from the supposed oppressive authoritarianism of the Catholic Church – propagated as having held back liberal civilization since the end of the Greco-Roman.

From this rejection of anything to do with the "old" religion of Christendom there was a revival of interest (renaissance) in the pagan world of science and literature (and art as well). Hume reveals he immersed himself in this pagan (classical) literature in which there was of course a variety of diverse and opposed philosophies, most of which opposed the superstitious form of the religions of pagan times. Amongst these philosophical schools, there was a strong strain of skepticism present as well. Hume spends some time considering them.

It is said that when his older brother went to Edinburgh University such was Hume's precociousness that his mother allowed him to go too, possibly at the age of 10 or 11. It was hoped that he would become a lawyer and he did the law course but found the idea of law as a profession distasteful ("nauseous" apparently was his own word). As put by an Internet source, "in his words, he came to have:'...an insurmountable aversion to everything but the pursuits of Philosophy and general Learning; and while [my family] fanceyed I was poring over Voet and Vinnius [apparently law books of the time], Cicero and Virgil were the Authors which I was secretly devouring.'"

What is worth noting is the fact that Hume produced the Treatise, really the *magnum opus* of his life (if refined by the *Enquiries*) in his twenties, from 24 to 28, after he had studied virtually unaided the vast literature involved.

We ought to make some observations on this feature of Hume's mental development and the way the modern mind has been formed. Aristotle had noted that where focused on Mathematics the young grasp the subject matter quickly and indeed there are many cases of prodigies in subjects in which Mathematics is an important part, such as music - think of Mozart.

So when the modern mind became focused generally on not physics so much as mathematical physics modern thinking and science were advanced at a rapid rate by those of a young age, with a certain contempt for their elders. As with Hume, the most prominent thinkers of modern times formed their grand systems of thought early and never really changed them over the rest of their lives. This made for a characteristic of modern philosophy of a disdain for tradition and authority, every generation tending to be dominated by a new "genius" with philosophical systems overtaking one another. The idea of a perennial philosophy was rejected *a priori* as necessarily simply an ossified old system (a similar assessment then was made of a religion that claimed to have lasted for going on one thousand six hundred years without essential change).

The focus on the particular mathematical and empirical sciences only reinforced this characteristic of modern thought. Metaphysics and the notion of wisdom as something higher than science were dismissed as at best "speculation" on matters that were unscientific, and therefore meaningless. This is the state of mind that Hume ended up in.

Hume has so influenced subsequent modern thinkers that despite his own description of his *magnum opus* as juvenile he is held up as "one of the most important philosophers to write in English". Indeed, his influence spread further than the English speaking world. The article on him in the Stanford University Encyclopaedia of Philosophy goes on to say: "Kant reported that Hume's work woke him from his 'dogmatic slumbers' and Jeremy Bentham remarked that reading Hume 'caused the scales to fall' from his eyes. Charles Darwin regarded his work as a central influence on the theory of evolution.... Today, philosophers recognize Hume as a thoroughgoing exponent of philosophical naturalism, as a precursor of contemporary cognitive science, and as the inspiration for several of the most significant types of ethical theory developed in contemporary moral philosophy."

We can see how the rejection of Metaphysics and Ethics as natural and practical wisdom might affect the human mind so as to produce a state of mental immaturity (there is a stronger word for lack of wisdom). We can also understand how Aristotle's explanation of this unwise state of scientific knowledge can be attributed to having a too narrow focus on the material world of change, as with Heraclitus, which we have noted can be related to the modern attempt to provide a general Theory of Evolution.

But we have also noted that there is a second source mentioned by Aristotle and that is the reduction of human philosophy to a matter of opinion. The logical discussion of fundamental and general questions is therefore reduced to a rational art lower than the Analytics of Aristotle, whose conclusions are able to be certain. On the other hand, Dialectic and Rhetoric (Sophistic is a related art to which Aristotle linked Protagoras) have conclusions that are less than certain. Though modern philosophers adopt the use of the words "Logic" and even "Analytic" they are in Aristotelian terms immersed in Dialectic, Rhetoric and especially Sophistic.

Here we can notice a concentration on words rather than things. Hume excused himself in using definitions of the words not in their "usual" sense. That is part of the problem with reading him, though we can detect where he is heading. But more significant is that Hume had a way with words (no doubt from his study of the classics). The Stanford University article notes that he "was also well known in his own time as an historian and essayist. A master stylist in any genre." This relates to the second source of error in fundamental philosophy Aristotle referred to.

It is important to note here that, though it was inherent in his focus first on human nature, Hume went from an interest in theoretical "metaphysical" matters to one in practical or political ones, where the "art of persuasion" is most useful. Most modern philosophers on close examination were and are more interested in Politics than anything else (even Kant and Hegel, Mill and Russell, Heidegger and Sartre, and of course Marx).

Thus, Hume's works were influential in both ways in forming the modern mind. Aristotle listed five rational arts (confused sometimes with "liberal arts") Analytic, Dialectic, Sophistic, Rhetoric and Poietic. We have dealt with them earlier and we will deal with them more fully in our next book in this series, "Logic, Science and Saint Thomas Aquinas". They all depend upon the use of words or language and we have noted how the modern mind has used especially Dialectic and Rhetoric (mixed with Sophistic), the former tending to be used in theoretical subject matters and the latter in practical.

It is this focus on words and language that is perhaps the most significant feature of modern philosophy. In order to bring out the modern method of "reasoning" we might note that the Greek root of the word for rhetoric is *rhe*, which means flow. It is in the word for the medical disorder diarrhoea. Not to make too much of an analogy between the physical and mental, there can be a similar disorder in the use of the art of rhetoric that may be applied to much modern discussion of philosophical subjects.

Then we have to consider the other characteristic of youth. The young mind, if allowed free rein, is more inclined to action (activism) than wisdom. This we may notice in Hume whose interest was turned from the study of the psychological side of human nature to the moral side in the sense of the practical political. The same may be noticed of Locke. Moreover, at the time, revolution was in the air, having grown in intensity from its religious beginning in the 1500's to the discontent with political authority in the late 1700's. Hume died only a short time before the French and American Revolutions.

The republican movement against monarchy reached a peak in England and took its form from the "Glorious Revolution" of 1688. However, the English were more adept at changing the substance of monarchy whilst keeping up appearances. This kept in the English "constitution" the trappings of monarchy in both the political and (Protestant) religious "establishment". There is more behind the "appearances" that we do not go into here. In the young USA whilst retaining for a time a protestant "low church" religious form the political revolution proclaimed itself as a republic by rejecting the monarchy, but here again there was more going on "behind the scenes" that the politico-economic structure of capitalism was anxious to keep hidden.

In both England, or Britain, or the UK, and the USA the "constitutions" became more "republican" (if more accurately oligarchical/capitalist, an effective rule of the "propertied" few, as we have explained). This was propagated "rhetorically" as democracy, and the propertyless working majority were indoctrinated to be thankful for the opportunity of employment and survival. In times where the greed of the fortunate few pushed wages to starvation levels the government came to the rescue and the unemployed could thank the State for its invention of a system of "social security", otherwise known as Social Welfare.

However, these are considerations that do not belong to the subject matter of this book. For they bring in practical/political aspects of the changes that ushered in the modern era. For our purposes we are concerned only with the first part of Hume's Treatise (to which we can relate his first Enquiry). We also need to leave out the treatment of the "passions". For, in his treatment of the passions Hume mixes up psychic states (not properly to be put under impressions) with strictly moral ones, displaying at the same time a complete ignorance of the difference between cognitive and affective aspects of human nature.

It may help to insert a short account of the distinctions made by Aristotle and Aquinas in regard to psychology and in particular human psychology. The basic distinction is between knowledge (cognition), which is the having by a knower of the forms of other things as well as its own, and the inclinations following such forms had, which in an animal are expressed in certain acts called love/hate, desire/aversion and joy/sadness where the thing is seen as simply good or bad, and called by other names where the thing is seen as mixed.

These psychic acts of appetite and affection are called "passions". The full treatment of them may be seen in our book "Psychology, Science and Saint Thomas Aquinas". We need only note here that Hume's treatment on Passions shows no understanding of the fundamental distinction between cognition and affection. For instance, he puts such psychic acts that should be treated under inclinations, following forms known, under the term "impressions", which is a kind of cognition.

So he lumps all sorts of things that he cannot put as sensations in a separate category of impressions called reflective. Then all these are opposed to ideas on the score of vividness and paleness, or forcefulness and weakness. Obviously, he is opposing psychic acts (confusing the cognitive with the affective) at the level of the external senses and sensuality to those at the level of the internal senses, so that "idea" does not differ from "image". (Locke and Berkeley had done the same). That way he can reduce all human psychology to the animal level of sense.

Hume's ignorance of Aristotle's masterly treatment of the higher internal senses of the animal, which includes man, can be seen in the complete failure of any reference to the third higher internal sense after imagination and memory, namely, the estimative sense. It is what we generally refer to as instinct. Other names for it were natural judgment and prudence, and even animal intelligence. Significantly, in man when acting under the influence of intellect it is called the cogitative sense. It is where most of the confusing of human and animal acts occurs. Obviously, Descartes did not know the difference between *cogito* and *intelligo*.

Hume's attribution of reason in animals as equivalent to human reason is owing to his ignorance of this facility in the higher animals. In a way, all his mistakes stem from this failure in being able to distinguish between human psychology as generally animal and as specifically rational. The fact that this was not picked up in subsequent history of modern philosophy can be explained from Hume not being alone in this ignorance and neglect of Aristotle's *Peri psyche*. The neglect, unfortunately, extends to modern Catholic psychologists.

We should note here that terms to do with the nature of human psychology, which had an intelligible sense in Aristotle and Aquinas, began to lose their definite meanings in the late scholastic age. But, from Descartes on, such words as "idea", "understanding" and "mind" lost almost completely their definite intent and became a muddle-headed confusion. Put shortly, we may say that the focus on Mathematics led Descartes to confuse the intellect's idea with the imagination's image. The British empiricists then had the problem of dealing with general and abstract ideas, to which we will come to below.

We can, however, attribute all this confusion to the loss of Metaphysics and the attempt to squeeze all human thought into the particularist boxes that were "natural science" and mathematics, or Newtonian Physics (mathematical physics). Thus, the two sources of error in Metaphysics, a narrow focus on the science of the material world and an entanglement in disputation around contradictory opinions, combined to produce the confused state of Hume's and the modern mind, and push it into radical skepticism not only in philosophy generally, but also and specially in the philosophy of science (now "grounded" in hypothesis).

This confusion of thought Descartes had earlier desired to cure by his call for "clear and distinct" ideas, but his notion of such was just to apply the mathematical mode of thinking to everything. That ended up with what came to be called "rationalism", which inevitably failed to clarify things.

British Empiricism, culminating in Hume, was an effort to achieve something of the same result by adopting the "experimental" side of the Newtonian scientific method. Hume, like J. S. Mill, was weak in Mathematics, and tried to see things exclusively through the lens of the experimental method. But here too the particularist focus on observation and experiment only exacerbated the confusion of thought and language. One has simply to look at his key words to illustrate this. We have seen his use of the word "moral". "Metaphysical", as he describes it, would equate with the subjects of Aristotle's dialectics (and sophistics).

The word "impression," which Hume divides into of sensation and of reflection, is a term of cognition. So too the word "perception" signifies in the case of sense a more complete or perfect kind of knowledge, which suggests the operation of the common sense, or sense consciousness. Impressions proper to an individual sense, such as of colour to sight, or of heat to touch, are receptions of singular objects of sense knowledge, but the common sense (sense consciousness) unifies them though distinct from each other in what we might call a perception.

Analogously, we can then refer to an intellectual apprehension, or better a judgment, as "perceptive". But having no understanding of the complex objects of sense consciousness, as distinct from individual impressions from one or other of the external senses, Hume puts under impressions "passions", appetites and affections. Strictly speaking, pleasure and pain should be put in the category of affections, not cognitions (impressions).

Hume obviously intended all human psychic life to be limited to the level of sense. In pairing "reflection" with sensation under the meaning of impression, Hume rubs out the distinction between affective acts, "passions", and cognitive ones. Then he resorts to the lowest level of the language of force to make the distinction between impressions and ideas. Ideas, are classed under perceptions, but, for the empiricists, have to be thought of as individual as images, products of the imagination. Hume then places memories somewhere in between images (ideas) and impressions (because of his division on the basis of forcefulness). To say the least, that is juvenile psychology. Nonetheless, it seems to be the level that "metaphysical"/philosophical discussion descended to after Newton.

This kind of crude materialist thinking and language was taken up in the New World, if initially more from Locke than Hume. It later descended even lower with the adoption of a debased commercial language (where do you think that came from?) in one of America's most celebrated "practical" philosophers William James, with his "cash value" criterion of truth. Generally then, this is the thinking that was most influential on the younger generations in England and on the Continent, and in the United States of America from the time of its foundation. Initially, not everyone in America was amenable to Hume's thinking because of its anti-religious character. But as the Protestant religion waned so did the influence of Hume wax.

That should be enough to say on Hume to show how he added (youthful) "force" to the undermining of our understanding and the certainties of and from metaphysical principles. Kant, to whom we will come shortly tried unsuccessfully to restore confidence in modern science, as Newtonian. But, the mental damage was too deep-rooted in the idealist presupposition and the rejection of Metaphysics.

It is not a matter of wonder therefore that one such as Hegel should arise to propose that reality was to be found identified with mentality and truth could be built on contradiction itself. Marx applied the Hegelian "dialectic" to the modern political world of conflict at the economic level, between the people of property (capitalists) the people without (workers).

Whilst the contemporary intellectuals have tried to do something with or against Hegel and Marx, the young have preferred to take "direct action", the results of which are painfully with us today. But this is looking a little ahead.

For the reasons given, it is only the first book of the Treatise that we need to focus on and then only on the First Part, so far as the subject matter of our book is concerned. Nor is it really necessary to consult the First Enquiry, as Hume himself affirms that the difference is not in "matter" but "manner". We have already made it clear where the fault in Hume's thinking lies. Let us look at three particular examples of his faulty thinking.

We treat first of what Hume says of ideas. "Now since all ideas are derived from impressions, and are nothing but copies and representations of them, whatever is true of the one must be acknowledged concerning the other. Impressions and ideas differ only in their strength and vivacity. The foregoing conclusion is not founded on any particular degree of vivacity. It cannot therefore be affected by any variation in that particular. An idea is a weaker impression; and as a strong impression must necessarily have a determinate quantity and quality, the case must be the same with its copy or representative."

The idea of horse (or triangle) then must have the same determinate quantity as the sense impression of a horse. It is a simple copy, like a drawing or picture. Putting aside for the moment that the horse that one has derived the idea from must be a bundle of impressions, not each of which will be the same quality or colour (maybe it is a black horse with a white stripe on its forehead), one's idea of horse must be exactly the same as the bundle of impressions, if a bit hazy.

Clearly, Hume is taking for his idea of horse the image of a particular horse he has seen. He must then have as many ideas of horse (in his imagination) as the impressions of individual horses have come within his experience. My idea of horse, on the other hand, has to be a number of diverse ideas according to my diverse experience of horses. Best of luck talking about horses at the racecourse.

As soon as one tests one's knowledge of impressions and ideas this is seen to be obvious nonsense. It is not even true of animal knowledge, using only sense impressions and images. For Hume has tried to explain these two kinds of knowledge without the two most important unifying ones, sense consciousness and "instinct". He thinks he can do what he does from the fact that all experience is individualized down to the multiple impressions that go to make up our knowledge of anything in nature. The first notion of idea then is but that of an individual image that represents what one has from one individual impression (wherever from).

This immediately gives rise to the problem of how to explain the fact that our ideas, indeed a multitude of them, are abstract or general. But this is really a jump that distracts us from the impossibility of even explaining the idea of horse as a unity. As expressed later, by William James, the content of one's mind is but a "stream of consciousness" (here's that flow again). Even the individual horse has to be a copy of impressions that are constantly changing, as colours in the light. The image/idea, insofar as it copies the complex of impressions, stays the same but for a moment.

From the standpoint of Hume's empiricist "explanation" there are no individual horses had in mind from which to abstract or generalize. But let's ignore this more basic problem and proceed as if some assert there is one horse understood because the human mind (imagination) abstracts from all the individual differences belonging to things in nature, and had in our impressions.

Hume is not satisfied with Locke's solution, which would have the mind ignoring individuating differences and focus somehow on what is left. But, Hume says, the individuating differences are what make up the ideas, just as they do the impressions, because that is how things exist. The abstract or general idea must be just as individual and concrete as things in nature. Fully analysed indeed they must represent the multiple and changing character of the complex of impressions we mistakenly refer to as one thing (horse).

However, here Berkeley comes to the rescue. Let Hume explain it: "A very material question has been started concerning ABSTRACT or GENERAL ideas, WHETHER THEY BE GENERAL OR PARTICULAR IN THE MIND'S CONCEPTION OF THEM. A great philosopher has disputed the received opinion in this particular, and has asserted, that all general ideas are nothing but particular ones, annexed to a certain term, which gives them a more extensive signification, and makes them recall upon occasion other individuals, which are similar to them. As I look upon this to be one of the greatest and most valuable discoveries that has been made of late years in the republic of letters, I shall here endeavour to confirm it by some arguments, which I hope will put it beyond all doubt and controversy."

The great philosopher is of course Berkeley who was most insistent that only qualities of mind existed, e.g. the impression or image/idea of a horse. There were no material things outside a mind. Thereby Berkeley believed he proved reality was spiritual, taking all knowledge, even sensitive (in fact all knowledge is reduced to same) as "immaterial".

Hume obviously did not go along with this final position of Berkeley, but he found the explanation of abstract and general ideas, which disposed of any notion that they were not images as concrete and individuated as ideas that were copies of singular impressions, as "one of the greatest and most valuable discoveries that has been made of late years in the republic of letters". The confirmatory arguments Hume refers to we will leave the reader to study. We see them as saying the same thing in different ways.

What it comes down to is taking a particular thing such as a statue of a soldier (unknown but recognizable as an individual) to stand for or represent all soldiers. It is not noticed, however, that the generality of the signification comes from the operation of an intellect where the product is individual as a work of art. The particular term referred to by Berkeley is then given without warrant the significative "virtue" of a work of art. Supposing a statue of a dog was made to represent all dogs, regardless of their individual/specific differences. It would have to be an individual dog What do you think a dog passing by would make of the statue, even if so life-like as to appear to be a real dog? Could it be made to stand for all dogs in its "mind"? The image or "idea" is supposed to perform the same sort of function. For Hume regards the human mind as constituted in the same animal way.

The exercise is just as successful as are all others whereby Hume tries to bolster up his position. With literary (rhetorical) skill he builds up a 'case" that is no more that a series of assertions that have a connection that he himself would regard as only "gentle". Examples of what are mere assertions are that there are complex impressions and ideas, when there is no idea given of what makes them so. This applies also to his "three laws of association", by resemblance, contiguity in time and place, and cause and effect. The second is but an expression of contingency from which nothing can be derived. The third is a relation of causality where Hume spends much effort in arguing that any connection involved is not empirically observable and therefore not rationally defensible.

For all this he asks us to go along with what he says. That might be being kind to Hume but not to philosophy or science. Here we end Chapter Three and move on to Immanuel Kant who does make use of Hume in another modern attempt to avoid radical skepticism and defend modern science.

Chapter 4

Kant

With Kant we move on to a shift in the modern philosophical scene in many and dramatic ways. Some of these can be put in social and cultural terms, in a shift from an Anglo-French context to a German one (though we should obviously take "anglo" not to mean simply English, or Anglo-Saxon, but to include Irish and Scottish and early American). In regard to thinking, the German experience of philosophy was formed first in the Cartesian "rationalist" mode, mainly because of Leibniz and those who were influenced by him. Newton was of course known not only for the controversy with Leibniz over who it was the first to discover the calculus, but already as the genius of modern science.

In his early intellectual life Kant was firmly in the line of such thought, from Wolff to Knutsen, and were it not for reading Hume he most probably would have stayed with that rationalist line. So we must put Kant as an exception to the general trend of early modern philosophers forming their systems as Hume did, in their relative youth. Kant had to revise drastically his thoughts in mid life and only developed his final system quite late.

He was an assiduous student and had early absorbed an enormous amount of learning not just in the new modern works that had come out since Descartes and Leibniz, which covered both science and philosophy, but also in ancient and mediaeval works. Unlike Hume his interest in the "classics" seems to have been more scientific than literary.

Nonetheless, his learning was prodigious and it may be noted that, also unlike Hume, his whole scholarly life was within a university, at Konigsberg, with an academic discipline that would be the envy of many. Study was his whole life, yet he was sensible enough to realize that he needed to have exercise and could be seen around Konigsberg taking his daily afternoon walk (with the locals, as the story goes, able to set their clocks by him). Whereas pictures of Hume show a man corpulent and rather unfit, those of Kant show a man lean and fit.

Another difference with Kant was his respect for religion even in a growing atmosphere of regarding science and religion as incompatible. He grew up in a family of Pietists (a branch of Lutheranism) and, though his thinking moved away from having a religious belief that could be founded in reason (even as natural religion), he evidently retained a need to make a place for religion in his life and thought. This had an effect on his explanation of the place of Metaphysics in his overall philosophy.

We do not need to go much more into the details of Kant's life and intellect and early influences, as the article on him in the Stanford University Encyclopedia of Philosophy is excellent in this regard, as it is generally on the development of Kant's philosophy over both his pre-critical and critical periods. Kant's intellectual background was quite extensive with much expertise in Newtonian science early. Kant was a mathematician and mathematical physicist of high class. This broadened to include practically every aspect of science and philosophy. Some indication of this may be had from the Stanford article:

"Kant attended college at the University of Königsberg, known as the Albertina, where his early interest in classics was quickly superseded by philosophy, which all first year students studied and which encompassed mathematics and physics as well as logic, metaphysics, ethics, and natural law. Kant's philosophy professors exposed him to the approach of Christian Wolff (1679–1750), whose critical synthesis of the philosophy of G. W. Leibniz (1646–1716) was then very influential in German universities. But Kant was also exposed to a range of German and British critics of Wolff, and there were strong doses of Aristotelianism and Pietism represented in the philosophy faculty as well. Kant's favorite teacher was Martin Knutzen (1713–1751), a Pietist who was heavily influenced by both Wolff and the English philosopher John Locke (1632–1704). Knutzen introduced Kant to the work of Isaac Newton (1642–1727), and his influence is visible in Kant's first published work, *Thoughts on the True Estimation of Living Forces* (1747), which was a critical attempt to mediate a dispute in natural philosophy between Leibnizians and Newtonians over the proper measurement of force."

For the purposes of our book we do not need to go further into the details of Kant's considerable scientific and philosophical output. What is really for us to do is assess Kant's critical philosophy from an Aristotelian viewpoint, and that only as it is relevant to the subject matter of our book. This virtually limits our concern to Kant's *Critique of Pure Reason*, though we will need to make some general comments on the relation between the three critiques.

One thing we need to bring out is that Kant apparently had some acquaintance with Aristotle's works, more so it would seem than Hume did. He probably also had a knowledge of scholasticism, including Aquinas. However, this would have had to be affected by the general tendency of the time to view scholasticism through the work of Suarez, rather than Aquinas

The key to understanding Kant's philosophy in fact is his use of the fundamental Aristotelian concepts of form and matter, distorted, as we shall see, by being used in the context of the modern subjectivist/idealistic presupposition, for which the works of the early Jesuits must bear some responsibility.

One can wade through the argumentation of Kant if one desires to argue for him or against him, but the misuse of the notions of form and matter can be quickly shown and all of his subsequent "reasoning" seen to be obviously defective. That it has received such positive reception and even acclamation from an admiring academia has a simple explanation. The audience is not a match for the magician on stage.

Let us look at how the trick is worked. First, we must understand the meanings of form and matter as explained by Aristotle. They are first applied to notions required by Aristotle to explain substantial change, as for instance when a horse dies. It had the substantial form of horse, what makes it a horse, and why we can identify all other like animals as horses. But how did it lose such substantial form?

The notion of form is not to be taken from the fact that all horses have a particular shape, though this is where Aristotle first takes the word "form" (*morphe*) from. It is what "makes" something a horse, something substantial which has a horse bite and kick. One may get to know a horse better by these actions, but one is not likely to say that a horse is nothing but a combination of horse shape, horse bite and horse kick and whatever belongs to a horse in this fashion.

For Aristotle there is something substantial "standing under" whereby we understand what a horse is. It is form taken in this primary sense that Aristotle wants us to understand the form of horse to be, even though this being does not act or appear except through its "accidents", such as the features we have referred to.

However, the being or substance of a horse is not something of pure form. Otherwise it would not have any reason to change or die. All material things besides having a substantial form are also required to have another internal substantial principle to account for the fact that they can undergo substantial change, as happens when the horse dies.

This other substantial principle Aristotle called primary matter. The word "matter" it seems Aristotle took from the example of shaped wood (*hylemorphe*). He saw the need to explain what is within a material thing that underlies a change of form by an example from art. For thereby we can readily see that the shape can remain the same but the "matter" change, or the material remain and a new form be acquired. This explains why the form of the horse can be lost and the matter takes on another substantial form, such as of grass when the horse dies.

Indeed, all sorts of physical change can be accounted for in this way. When the horse eats grass the form of grass is lost and its matter acquires the form of a horse. But we will not go into these various kinds of change involving the union within things bodily of form and matter. They are called substantial form and primary matter, but we could just as well call them primary form and substantial matter.

Modern thinkers have no idea of how to understand the words used for form and matter, and especially substantial form and primary matter, as they were originally explained by Aristotle, and understood properly for over a thousand years. The very use of them properly was thrown out as part of "Metaphysics". And when Kant reintroduced their use it was in the subjectivist/idealist context of a pseudo-metaphysics.

Our understanding of material things depends upon identifying forms. Aristotle points out that primary matter is pure potency, and cannot be understood by itself. It can only be understood as related to form. That is to say, of itself, it is unintelligible. This is important to remember when we come to compare Kant's use of form and matter. In effect, Kant applies this notion of matter to what is secondary matter, a most general concept of bodies actually existing with one form or another,

That is to say Kant took the content of the material order of things (real horses etc.) outside the mind, as equivalent to Aristotle's notion of primary matter. Kant has evacuated material reality of its natural forms, lumping together, minerals, plants, animals and human bodies as knowable only through *a priori* forms within the mind, and these *a priori* forms put in the most generic terms of space and time, categories of judgments, causality and so on. Plato had a more intelligible notion of forms.

One may gather at this stage what has gone wrong with his use of the traditional distinction between form and matter. It is glaring to an Aristotelian, but the modern mind has ditched Aristotle. That misuse of the notions of form and matter however should be enough to dismiss the whole of Kant's "Copernican Revolution".

But what is to be noticed is that there is a certain convenient parallelism between Kant's union of form and matter and the union of form and matter in physico-mathematical science. In this order of sciences the mathematical form is in a way imposed on the empirical material so that what is internal in imagination is used to order what is "external" in sense impressions. For St. Thomas explains that in these medial sciences the mathematical part is as form to the physical part as matter.

There is no doubt that this aspect of Newtonian science was at the forefront of Kant's thinking as he struggled to reconcile the opposite ways the modern understanding of human knowledge had developed along a "rationalist" (mathematical) line from Descartes (and Leibniz) and an "empiricist" (physical) line from Locke (and Hume). The duality of these subjectivist lines of thought came from misunderstanding the fact that human knowledge is not purely intellective, nor purely sensitive, but a union of the two.

The modern mind, mesmerized by Kant's magic, accepted, at least for a time, that he had solved the problem posed by Hume, by attributing his skeptical conclusion to the matter of pure empirical experience. (Newtonian) Science then is not concerned with any supposed real intelligible world outside the mind (whatever it may mean) – the idealist presupposition having been absorbed - but with the union of this material order of things as matter and the *a priori* forms provided by the mind, which union Kant called phenomena. The notion of the object of science being "phenomenon" (from Gk. for appearance) entered the language of modern science as quite congenial with the notions of there being no certainty obtainable in science, whose laws are ultimately hypothetical, not categorical (the latter a notion that, significantly and incongruously, Kant reserved for the practical/moral part of his philosophy).

Here we may pause to note that Kant's misuse of the notions of form and matter is so basic as to make his subsequent assertions nothing but a contrived work of imaginative art, built upon the false foundation of the subjectivist/idealist presupposition that had captured the new notion of science essentially focused on the physico-mathematics of Newton.

With the loss of Metaphysics, substance and all notion of reality outside the human mind had "disappeared". An attempt to found human knowledge on Mathematics alone (terminating in imagination) had taken the modern philosophers to one dead end. An attempt to found it on empirically based knowledge alone (terminating in sensation) had taken it to the alternative dead end. That is where Kant came into the "crisis".

Not able to understand how Metaphysics fitted into the scheme of theoretical science Kant hit upon the idea of somehow providing a synthesis that would preserve the unity of modern science. Aristotle's combination of form with matter (or act with potency) is the only one that does make something one. Indeed, physico-mathematical science, as explained by Aquinas, is one science. Kant evidently saw the use of these notions of form and matter as a clue to overcoming the contradictory opposition that modern thought had fallen into.

He failed to take notice of the subjectivist capture referred to and the loss of a metaphysical grasp of reality. In his *Critique of Pure Reason* he was prepared to ditch Metaphysics as a natural wisdom superior to the particular sciences of Mathematics and Physics, but hoped to save it somehow in the form of practical wisdom. But all subsequent "construction" of his philosophical system falls to the ground with the retreat from reality in the way he used the Aristotelian notions of form and matter in the first critique.

That subjectivist misuse is enough to make his whole project without foundation. There is really no need to enter into the details of his other two critiques. However, the mistaking of the meanings of form and matter, though the most fundamental in the collapse of the Kantian enterprise, is not the only misuse of Aristotelian concepts used by Kant on his way through his critical philosophy. He makes a right mess of the notion of reason itself, obviously central to his argument.

To appreciate this we need to set out shortly Aristotle's exposition of human intellectual knowledge. Primarily, this knowledge (cognition) is the work of the human spiritual soul through its power called intellect. Sometimes this power or faculty is also called the reason. But we have to be careful here, for reason can not only be used as equivalent to intellect but also as a lesser function than intellect acting as intellect.

To see this we need to set out the three acts of the human intellect, apprehension, judgment and reasoning. So we have to distinguish intellect acting as intellect and acting as reason (reasoning).What is to be noticed immediately here is how Kant has misused the notions of *a priori* and *a posteriori*, which apply only to reasoning. Kant has made them apply to judgments and introduced a strange notion of *a priori* synthetic judgments to account for the necessity of mathematical propositions as distinct from the contingency of purely empirical ones (*a posteriori*). We will not go into this peculiarity, but it is something that Kant saw as highly significant in his notion of science.

Each of the three acts has a product, concept or idea, proposition or statement and proof. They also can be divided into formal and material parts, the concept into the form of universality and the matter of objective content, the proposition into the form of attribution or predication and the matter of the truth or falsity of the proposition (the difference between analytic and dialectic complicates this) and the reasoning into the form of validity and the matter of consequent truth (or falsity).

Many confuse universality with the condition of a concept as abstract. But it is the object of the concept that is abstract (e.g. the form or nature of horse which is the same form without its individuality as that in the real individual horse) and universality is a logical property. Formal Logic is concerned with these logical forms or properties and they exist only in the mind. It is this exclusively mental state of the parts of human intellectual knowledge that the modern mind gets mixed up on. That is not to say that there was no confusion in this regard in pre-modern times and especially in late scholasticism.

These necessary distinctions will be more fully dealt with in our next book. One may appreciate, however, how mixed up the modern mind can get without the help of Aristotle and Aquinas. Kant was just a superior mental contortionist. He takes the word "reason" and runs with it as if it were the same as "understanding", which is the word for human knowledge that Locke and Hume used. But, as St. Thomas notes, "understanding" can be taken in three ways, first for the power of intellect (where reason is sometimes used), second for the act of judgment, and third for the habit of first principles, necessarily true, such as the principle of non-contradiction.

Kant opposes pure reason to practical reason when the proper opposition is between natural wisdom and practical wisdom. Pure reason, as intended by Kant, cannot rise above mathematical concepts and reasoning. Practical Reason, however, as wisdom has to rise above the level of pure reason conceived by Kant and so he puts it above reason, as faith. But, by faith Kant cannot mean Christian faith. His meaning is something contrary to reason, or at best mere human faith, what Aristotle called opinion.

That is enough to dispose of the second critique. Its focus is on morality, but a morality unsupported by (theoretical) reason. Yet Kant introduces language that makes it appear to have more certainty than reason, such as its first imperative being called categorical and not hypothetical, the second condition that Aristotle puts for the principle of non-contradiction.

Then, in the third critique he introduces the notion of judgment as somehow tied to end and the beautiful. This again is a misuse of the notion of judgment, which has to be part of every intellectual process in science and philosophy.

There are a host of other incongruous standpoints taken in the first critique, whose very study is a laborious exercise. But, as noted above, such detailed examination is unnecessary once having detected the critique's fundamental flaw. It was no doubt an honest and sincere attempt to overcome the consequences of the wrong turning made by the modern mind and the loss of the philosophical wisdom of Aristotle, as expounded upon by Aquinas. This inevitably followed upon the rejection of the divine authority of the Catholic Church and, as we have also noted, had its roots in the will before the intellect. We do not go into the theological consequences, though many modern philosophers, for example Hegel and Marx, have mixed in theological concepts from their Protestant and Judaic backgrounds. Heidegger caused havoc in Catholic theology.

The 1700s saw a veritable outburst of enthusiasm for what appeared to be a new age of enlightenment and triumph of the human spirit. Exploration both physical and mental was engaged in and promoted at almost fever pitch. The sense of a new found freedom or autonomy was everywhere in European civilization, having thrown off the social and religious incubus of a previous hidebound world. This was manifested not only in secular terms but also in the new religious (protestant) ones. It was the age of Wesley as well as that of Wolff.

Kant drew upon all the diverse scientific and philosophical movements of his time, even religious (there being some connection between Pietism and Methodism). All recognize a profound influence on him of Rousseau who was a precursor of the philosophy of Romanticism that followed that of the Enlightenment. This is marked by the promotion of human will over intellect or reason, which brings out more radically the roots of the modern mind. Hume, indeed, had some element of this. As we have seen he put the passions before reason.

Kant's mind may be seen as a kind of watershed into which the major lines of division especially in philosophy that had arisen following the end of Christendom were collected together and an attempt made to make them one again, but what occurred in fact was a turning point for the previous divided waters to be redirected in similar but more turbulent streams. We have already noted the division of the human mind into intellect and will, which may be reflected in the distinction the ends of knowledge for its own sake and for the purpose of action (and production). Human knowledge for its own sake is divided into intellect and sense, which makes for two streams merging in Kant. We will bring out below the fact that human knowledge for the sake of action can also be seen as forming two streams, personal and political. So it is that modern philosophy after Kant takes four basic forms. Rationalism and Empiricism turns into Idealism and Positivism. We have yet to discuss the courses of Liberalism and Socialism after Kant.

It is to be noted that Aristotle and Aquinas give priority in ultimate terms to knowledge (so that happiness is primarily a vision, though not to be had without joy). But in this life practical thinking is not less important than theoretical and we have noted it has a certain priority so far as the human condition is concerned. So it is that much of human philosophy is focused on practical affairs, especially ethics and politics. That brings in the will, and we must not forget that the rejection of the divine authority of the Catholic Church and Faith is a matter of choice, personal fundamentally, but not without social repercussions.

It is the political that dominates the discussion of practical life and affairs, though in late scholasticism it was the theological importance of the personal that was prominent in the thinking in such as Scotus (with his voluntarism). But the focus on the political was not absent from the arguments about the rights of Church and State in Occam, and even incidentally in Dante.

However, in the early modern period the focus was on the theoretical and the supposed superiority of modern science over the pre-modern. Hence it is that Descartes is considered the father of modern thought and Newton the champion of modern science. The theoretical nature of the modern scientific method in fact tended to dominate all discussion even in practical affairs. (Note the history of modern economics and politics.) It should not be forgotten, however, that both Francis Bacon and Rene Descartes saw science as ordered to practical ends and human improvement, if in technical rather than ethical terms.

Kant followed this line of putting the practical above the theoretical, and he was thinking in terms of the practical/moral. Though he wished to save the sovereign status of science, it was a science that was limited to the physico-mathematical order of knowledge that could not go beyond the material order of sensible things. Incidentally, modern scientists understandably were not unhappy with this solution, in that it relegated human spiritual life to an objectively unverifiable individual/personal sphere. The Protestants, too, were possibly content to take "faith" as one's private interpretation of Scripture. Kant may have been thinking along these lines, but such a notion of "blind faith" is alien to Catholic thought.

Nonetheless, there was a deeper commitment in Kant's overall philosophy to the line of practical thinking, both in regard to personal ethics and social ethics, or politics, though it was closely knit with his theoretical philosophy. All commentators on Kant note that his leading idea was that of autonomy. This Kant applied first to human reason in its *a priori* conditions. Let us look briefly how he did this.

The two *a priori* or transcendental conditions in the case of sensibility Kant named space and time. This is how Kant put it in the case of space. "Space then is a necessary representation à priori, which serves for the foundation of all external intuitions. We never can imagine or make a representation to ourselves of the non-existence of space, though we may easily enough think that no objects are found in it. It must, therefore, be considered as the condition of the possibility of phenomena, and by no means as a determination dependent on them, and is a representation à priori, which necessarily supplies the basis for external phenomena."

Thus Kant makes the mind autonomous, or the self the ruler of the empirical data coming from our sensations, i.e. from the knowledge of sensibility. Without the *a priori* forms there can be no science, indeed, the things of experience outside the mind, without being "formed" by what is internal to the mind, are unknowable. It is the *a priori* condition of space that Kant makes the basis of Geometry.

How do Aristotle and Aquinas see this? Well, shortly put, Kant has got things back the front. What we first know are objects or forms in things that make impressions on our senses of sight and touch, such as colour and heat. But the things (bodies) are quantitative, and so the objects are limited in quantity, size, degree etc. We first experience things through their sensible objects (forms) and only after are they received in our imagination, as images or re-presentations. The objects of natural science are on the first level of intellectual abstraction and the objects of Mathematics are on the second level. Kant gives priority to the latter; like Descartes he lives in his imagination. It is just to be kept in mind that mathematical abstraction is concerned only with representing the quantitative aspect of things.

Aristotle says that we can abstract for the purpose of understanding bodies in two ways, which St. Thomas explains gives us the intelligible objects of natural science and of mathematics. The first way (from individual matter) keeps such an understanding of the sensible body (horse) that provides for it having necessary sensible qualities such as some colour and even some quantitative shape, but not determined to the individual (in the abstract concept of horse there is what St. Thomas calls "common matter").

The other way (called the second degree of abstraction) gives us the intelligible objects of mathematics, so that only the quantitative aspect of things is kept. What Aristotle called "sensible matter" is dropped, but not all matter. One finds difficulty in naming what is left. Aristotle called it "intelligible matter", but we would prefer to call it purely imaginable matter, since what we call "sensible matter" relates to all the objects of the external senses.

But what is important here is to realise that the imagination in forming images that are purely quantitative does not draw them out of the air but is fundamentally dependent upon abstracting the quantitative aspect of things from what has been presented to us by the external senses.

The mathematician is not supposed to lose touch with reality though there is, as in all sciences, much use of purely logical objects, such as the mathematical use of negative numbers. The notion of space, as of pure extended quantity, can only be imagined. Extended quantity has no sensible existence except in the physical universe of bodies, which Aristotle says is finite since no body can be infinite. The notion of space outside the physical world is therefore, as Aquinas says, something purely imaginary.

The same applies to time "before" creation. The modern mind, of course, dominated by Mathematics and taking the objects of its imagination "for real" fulfils Shakespeare's description of "man, proud man, ... most ignorant of what he's most assured ... plays such fantastic tricks before high heaven as make the angels weep". (Measure for Measure).

But, let us return to the turning point that is Kant's work. Rationalism turned into full Idealism and Empiricism turned into Positivism. The word "positivist" was originally applied to the new notion of theoretical sciences, (cf. Comte), but as we have seen the "scientific method" came to be applied generally to all modern studies whether theoretical or practical (as in the creation of new sciences of economics, law and politics.

Any practical moral or ethical principles or concepts, such as of justice, were deliberately excluded (as private value judgments). For, justice in the case of Politics was substituted power and self-interest or "profit" in the case of Economics. In the study of Law or Jurisprudence the notion of positive law took over from natural law. (One may notice how convenient this was to the politico-economic system of Capitalism, which could justify the dominance of the propertied few by the new Economic Science and enforce compliance with the established order by seemingly morally neutral political and legal means.)

The modern picture of how the new philosophical and scientific streams that flowed out of Kantianism is therefore somewhat complex. The development of German Idealism was quite clear and immediate. Fichte developed his version in the lifetime of Kant and met him. Indeed, he seemed to have been favourably considered and his early work was initially taken as of Kant himself.

It did not take long for the subjectivist/idealistic nature of Kant's philosophy to blossom into full Idealism. If the thing in itself was unknowable, why talk about it? The reality of the world external to the human mind together with any notion of physical matter went out the window. The philosophy of Idealism completed by Hegel swept all before it. During the 1800s Hegel virtually ruled the world of modern philosophy.

Positivism in science was promoted, by Comte and J.S. Mill, but as a philosophy had to take a back seat until a reaction against Hegel came about towards the end of the century. Interestingly, Bertrand Russell (godson of J. S. Mill) was initially a devotee of Idealism (which had conquered English philosophy for a time) but reacted against it to be a major figure in the newly fashioned (logical) empiricism/positivism of the early twentieth century (1900s). We omit here the practical/moral line taken by Mill and Russell (come from Hume through Bentham) called Utilitarianism, in which there was the twofold aspects of individualism and socialism.

But, we are getting a bit ahead of ourselves. We should only note here that the practical (purported moral) side of Kantianism, influenced by Rousseau, in which the autonomy of the human will is the leading idea, also has two streams, one individualist and the other socialist. The foundation of both is in an exaltation of individual human will, rejecting the natural moral law, where autonomy means being a law unto oneself.

A problem arises, however, in the social context, and particularly with political authority. How is the freedom of the individual to be reconciled with subjection to any kind of superior authority?

Aristotle and Aquinas faced the same problem. The individual person is possessed of free will. And so far as political society is concerned it is a rule of the free, and any political constitution has to be a form of self-rule (autonomous). But such human freedom is rooted in reason and truth. So the human person is free only when he acts in accord with his rational nature, which is expressed in the natural moral law "written in his conscience".

Aristotle then says that man is by nature social (a political animal). Thus, provided he submits freely to a constitutional rule that is in accord with his nature (Aristotle lists three) he remains free and achieves the true desires of his heart. The modern solution, in love with the idea of autonomy as free will taken absolutely, dismisses the notion of a natural moral law based on human rational nature.

So it is that all, Hobbes, Locke, Rousseau etc. endeavour to preserve individual autonomy by some sort of theory of social contract or agreement by all. What in Rousseau appealed to Kant was his notion of a general or universal will, in which each individual will was in some mystical way claimed to be actualized. This has carried through in more modern times to underlie the notion of democracy.

However, we do not wish to go any further here into this question, as it does not primarily belong to the subject matter of our book, which is to do with Metaphysics rather than Ethics. We will come to it more fully in our last book (12) of this series.

We might only mention that the modern position regarding human freedom, or practical autonomy, whether taken in its individualistic or socialistic form, is totalitarian. For, without adherence to the moral law, in the final analysis it matters not whether political rule is by one will (Hitler), or by a majority of wills (modern democracy), who make laws for all. Even if the majority (51%) are perfectly free themselves, there is such a thing as a tyranny of the majority. There is plenty of evidence of this in recent times.

We must take that as enough said of Kant's philosophy as it concerns the subject matter of our book. His influence on subsequent thinking has of course been enormous, as may be gathered from what we have already brought out. Insofar as subsequent systems of philosophy generally and explanations of the nature of science depend upon him they too must be judged to be equally deficient. To a certain extent then we may regard our task in this book as done. However, we will spend some time on the history of modern philosophy since, so as to bring our treatment as close to up to date as we can. Hopefully, we can keep this within one further chapter (5), which follows.

Chapter 5

After Kant

There are four streams of modern philosophical thinking that we can discern were in existence before Kant and which we contend were transformed by his attempt to make of them a unified whole. Two are in the field of theoretical knowledge, and two in the field of practical knowledge. We can name them provisionally Rationalism, Empiricism, Liberalism and Socialism.

These are all errors that appealed in some way to rationality and science. They all came to be in some way or other related to what is called the Enlightenment. But there is another current that so exalts will that it rejects reason altogether and in modern times has become anti-science. We can provisionally call it Romanticism.

Since all are names for errors, or in modern terminology ideologies, it is difficult to form a definite concept of them. For, as with evils, there is formlessness attached to their notions. They can only be understood relatively in terms of the goods they take away. Indeed it may be seen that the names are taken from notions that are good, such as reason, sense experience, freedom and society, and even will as such, which notions are used deceptively by the ideologues to justify their positions. Thus, it is that the terms are somewhat "slippery", and can be taken advantage of.

It is well to understand that the attention and even prominence given to human will is not essentially anti-rational. When
St. Thomas defines law for instance he says it is "of reason", but
with an act of will presupposed. It is to be remembered that Aristotle includes Poietics, i.e. what today we call literature, arts,
drama, the novel and the like, with which Romanticism is closely
allied, among the rational arts.

It is in the cultivation of these arts that humans are most affected by the goods (and evils) that pull or repel us to act or "re-
act". Brought into play are all the emotions, from love and hate to
fear and anger. None of these are necessarily opposed to reason
and virtue. But we have also to take into account the human condition of original sin and its effects, which, since the open rejection of the Church of Christ, from which the modern age defines
its personal and political freedom, seem if anything to be more
depraved than ever.

It seems that with "romantic" disorder (in the philosophical
sense) goes mental derangement of some sort. Kant tried to incorporate Rousseau into his "synthesis". After Kant, and Hegel,
there came Nietzsche. All these streams, being errors, and ex-
tremes, are at war with one another. Nonetheless, they find affinity with others in some respects. Liberalism and Socialism for
instance, find some affinity with Romanticism. Comte and Marx,
of whom we need to say something here in as much as they claim
the status of modern scientist, are examples, like Kant himself, of
throwing everything into a great "stew" in which there is something for every modern's taste (and, correspondingly, distaste).

However, let us try to "unscramble the egg" to some extent. One thing to note in regard to philosophy and science is that the theoretical errors were more prominent before Kant, whilst the practical were not so much in focus. The explanation for this most probably is that the practical order of things human was initially embroiled in theological concerns and it was not till some time after the religious wars were settled (circa 1650) that focus was then more clearly turned on to the problem of political control of individual free wills of human persons, and the practical/political ideologies of liberalism and socialism came to the surface.

Indeed, the use of the term "socialism" did not come into fashion till after Kant's death. It seems that a follower of Saint-Simon first used it in 1832. The practical/moral problem is of course inherent in human nature, especially as subject to original sin. Plato had to contend with it. Aristotle resolved it philosophically, but that did not remove it as a permanent source of conflict for the human condition, even after the coming of Christ.

Liberalism takes on a special religious significance since the beginning of the modern era with the Protestant revolt against the divine authority of the Catholic Church. The perceived opposition between the freedom of the individual and authority was correspondingly greatly intensified by religious fervor. The decline of Protestantism meant a lessening of this religious intensity, but the animus against authority remained and shifted to the exercise of authority generally and particularly political authority.

The century following the death of Kant, the 1800s, was one of utmost turmoil, not just in the actual social, economic and political, situation, but also in human thought. Remembering that it followed upon the French and American Revolutions, it was an age of revolution in every way. This mood of revolution began in Europe but spread to the rest of the world where European power and influence might be found. And the philosophical thinking in which we are primarily interested became almost impossibly complicated.

This applied even if one considered only Idealism. If you think that Kant's system of thought was complicated, just try to make sense of Hegel, who built his philosophy on identifying the rational and the real, even to the point of making contradiction the fundamental law of things.

The difference between the theoretical and the practical disappeared in his system of the Absolute. We can discern the transformation from Rationalism to Idealism through Kant, but it was more a transmogrification, the creation of a monster, a philosophical Frankenstein. Here we should advert to the use of the dialectic of Hegel by Karl Marx. From the point of view of Epistemology, which is our focus in this book, Marx's philosophy simply adopted the same errors as Hegel and so we do not need to add anything further in this regard. For his critique of Capitalism and the practical consequences (world shattering) of his version of Communism the reader can refer to our earlier books on Economics, Ethics and Politics.

However, so far as the Idealism that enters into modern philosophy in the 1800s is concerned, we should pause to point to a profound (Aristotelian) truth that could add force to this location of reality, as we know it, as totally within and from the human mind. But the nature of the human mind conceived by Kant and completed by Hegel was a total distortion. One does not have to read very far into both of these modern philosophers to see how gross their "creations" of human life and knowledge were. Diabolically, however, they gave the impression of saying something profound.

The fault lay not only in being captured by the idealistic presupposition of the modern mind, but more in operating intellectually at the lower level of mathematics and physics, and then trying to deal with metaphysical questions using such limited concepts and principles.

However, if Kant had been able to elevate his intellect to the metaphysical level of Aristotle and Aquinas (instead of being imprisoned in his fascination for Mathematics and Physicomathematics) he might have seen how the distinction of Aristotle into form and matter could have been made at a higher level, at the same time saving the intelligibility of the external world of things.

In our book "Psychology, Science and Saint Thomas Aquinas" we have explained Aristotle's exposition of human intellectual knowledge by drawing an analogy with how the power of sight operates. So far as the external object is concerned there are three "things" needed, the body (horse) and its colour (in its surface). But the colour is only visible if illuminated by light.

So ultimately it is light activating the form of colour of the body that makes an impression of the same form in the animal's organ of sight, which itself is a special kind of form, the (vital) power of sight. So the external world has a role to play in providing the forms of things to inform the knower. But the knower, though passive at this lower physical level is not inactive in cognitively assimilating the form (of colour) being received.

Indeed, just as we have seen that the living thing operates, immanently, at a higher level in assimilating food to maintain its bodily existence, so that we can say that a horse nourishes itself from hay, so the animal informs itself in the process of receiving the forms sensibly from the external things. But what is important to note so far is that what is material and acting physically, as light and illuminated colour in bodies, are a (instrumental) cause of knowledge. Without this causality coming from what is external to the knower there can be no knowledge at all (just as if there is no quality in a body to be illuminated there is nothing visible).

So we can say, with Hume, that our human knowledge, as animals, is totally dependent upon our sensations. But, using the example of light, we can divide this dependence into two. Without light we cannot see; and without a body with the capacity to be illuminated by light (the form of colour, potential/receptive to light) we cannot see a body. We do not see a horse or cow that is perfectly transparent; we see through them until the light reaches (is reflected from) a body that has a quality (opaqueness) that can "condition" the light to the level amenable to our power of vision.

The animal too has to have organs that are material but at a higher level than not just non-living bodies, but also than non cognitive ones. Even at this level of consideration of knowledge and life the modern scientist, looking through the lens of physico-mathematics, misses all the fine distinctions needed, and reduces his concept of matter to the lowest level. There we find that the objects are most accommodating to mathematical measurement. This is not to deny the usefulness of such knowledge.

In applying this analogy of the object of the sense of sight to the level of intellectual knowledge we only wish to note here that the human intellect has two functions, and goes by two names, active or agent intellect and potential or receiving intellect. Aristotle's word for the former is *nous poietikos*, which means "making intellect". But the activity is not to be conceived materialistically, nor too much efficiently as "agency".

It is a higher kind of activity, just as light has a higher kind of activity to say heat, or force. Thus, the other name for the agent intellect is light of understanding. This all becomes important to keep in mind when we attribute to the agent intellect the power of abstraction, which is that whereby the sensible image in the imagination is raised to the level of being able to be received into the potential intellect. Scholastic terminology can be quite confusing here, for it refers to the imagination sometimes as the passive intellect.

Now, we may be able to appreciate that all our knowledge can be explained internally, just as light contains all colours, but in such a higher way that the objects are invisible. The light has to be "filtered" by being incorporated in the potencies of the qualities of bodies that are proportioned to its reception. So too in intellectual knowledge only by the combination of these two sources of knowledge, in this case one completely internal, the other completely external, can the external things/forms be understood.

It only needs to be appreciated that God is the cause of our knowledge in two ways, as the cause of things and as the cause of the light of our understanding. The proofs for the existence of God, however, proceed more evidently from the things of the world in which we live.

By falling for the proposition that what we know are our own ideas (or impressions) the modern mind had closed off not only the connection with the real world outside but also a rational way to God. There would also be no means of communicating with other human beings. There may have felt to be a mystical internal connection with the divine but, from a natural point of view, it would have to be like looking directly at the sun.

There would of course be the knowledge of God by divine Faith and Revelation. But this is not meant to be without evangelization. However, these are all consequential matters that need to be explored elsewhere. It is enough for the purposes of our book to show the falsity and even absurdity of the idealist presupposition and the lowering of our sights.

German Idealism was the most obviously "rational" position to come out of Kantianism and it did so almost immediately in a progression from Fichte through Schelling to Hegel. The attempt to incorporate Humean empiricism as a source of human knowledge coming somehow from outside the mind was an abject failure, and seen to be so by the champions of Idealism.

Yet, ironically, Idealism as finally presented by Hegel, which virtually ruled the modern world of philosophy throughout the 1800s, was the most blatantly absurd of all intellectual positions. For an Aristotelian it takes less time to prove this than it did for showing up the basic falsity of Kant's philosophy. For the fault appears right at the beginning and, once understood, the rest of the system can be dismissed without further ado.

Hegel unashamedly put his original triad (equivalent to thesis, antithesis and synthesis) in what seemed to be metaphysical, even Aristotelian, terms as Being, Non-Being and Become. The first two expressed a contradictory opposition, which even in dialectical contests, where they are relevant as standing for positions taken by two separate opponents, has no possibility of compromise or "synthesis".

They cannot stand together in one mind, as Aristotle had shown in his treatment of the principle of non-contradiction, let alone have any possibility of existing together in the real. Hegel has misread Aristotle in his explanation of become or change, where he may use the expression "non-being" for "non actual being" as potency.

Hegel makes such a use of the denial of the principle of non-contradiction as would make Heraclitus blush. He builds his whole philosophy on this use of contradictory opposition, the language of which he tends to apply to the other kinds of opposition, privative in practical matters, and contrary in theoretical matters, where the main focus is on the physical order of change (become). Particular parts of his whole system may accommodate a valid point or a true conclusion. But there is little point in going into details such is the distorted foundation upon which the system is (imaginatively) constructed.

Nonetheless, there was much intellectual effort expended, and ink spilt, in efforts to refute his idealist absolutism. The use of the phrase "Absolute Spirit" brought the theists and even Christians into the fray. Famous names such as Soren Kierkegaard and Gabriel Marcel appealed to the order of existence to counter Hegel's Logical Essentialism. We do not propose to enter into these discussions here, as they would take us too far afield. What we can observe shortly is, that these modern thinkers were taking the notion of essence as used by Hegel too readily, as if he were a metaphysician.

Very few modern thinkers, even the least affected by modern compulsory but free education escape the influence of the subjectivist/idealist presupposition and the loss of a clear grasp of metaphysical principles. This in fact is the context in which Hegel's philosophy plays out, despite its metaphysical pretensions.

Husserl's effort, came to be called Phenomenology, influenced by Brentano, a Catholic ("ex?") priest with a good knowledge of

Aristotle, comes closest to restoring Aristotle's understanding of reality and our knowledge of it. But Husserl came from the modern mathematico-empirical background and saw his effort as a restoration in some fashion of Descartes's logico-objective thinking in order to overcome the psychologico-subjective notion of modern science. We will say something about this below when we look at the other transformation from Kant, from empiricism to positivism.

There is much more to say about the thinkers of the 1800s (and into the 1900s)who developed Hegel's philosophy or reacted against it, and also those who attempted to develop in other ways Kant's philosophy, called Neo-Kantians. But we do not wish to go further into their thinking, nor do we need to. It is enough to have established the fundamental flaws in Kant and Hegel upon which they attempted to build their own systems of thought.

We should turn now to **Positivism**, the other main line of thinking that came after Kant and, though not so directly attributable to his "revolution" as Idealism, did nonetheless adapt Kant's idea of modern science being more complex than pure empiricism could account for. Basically, however, philosophically it was a return to Hume and in the end it was accepted that the formal laws of science were no more than hypothetical (though for a time there was confidence that they were dealing with laws as fixed as Newton's: see discussion below in this regard).

Aristotle's and Kant's desire for "final" certainty in science was a mistaken one. The radical skepticism entailed in Hume's conclusions was shrugged off as insufficient to worry about in the face of the evident advance of science following Newton's scientific revolution. The philosophers of science could speculate as much as they liked, but the scientific method was proved by its results, the application of which method spread rapidly to every field of enquiry and produced astounding results. The philosophy behind Positivism thus rested to a great extent on Pragmatism, a notion that American philosophers in particular, such as William James, promulgated. A scientific finding can be considered true (enough) if it "worked".

We should note that the rise of Positivism involved in a way a kind of reverse cultural move to what had occurred in the case of Idealism, the centre moving from Germany back to France and England (Comte and J.S. Mill). Though not too much should be made of it, we can see the beginnings of what later became a sharp rift between "English" philosophy (refer to remarks above about "English" philosophy) and "Continental", reflecting remotely the original opposition between Rationalism and Empiricism, or Descartes and Hume, and coming to a head, as it were, in the contrasting content and styles of Heidegger and Wittgenstein, though ironically the latter was an Austrian who early moved to England.

A lot of water has to flow under the bridge over the English Channel before the interactions between the two basic approaches to modern philosophy can be sorted out, and we do not intend to attempt the task here, resembling as it does trying to draw one spaghetto at a time from a bowl of spaghetti (such exercises will keep young academics occupied for years to come).

It first has to be said that Idealism was strong during the 1800s in England (Bradley, Green and McTaggart) and even in USA (Royce) as Positivism was gaining ground. We have yet to note the complicated character positivism took. Then as Idealism fell out of favour at the end of the century (from critiques of Moore and Russell) all this was in the midst of a new series of sciences being created, a new physics, new economics, new logic and even new mathematics (the latter two forerunners of modern computers).

Russell moved from Idealism not to the Positivism of Mill but, being a mathematician, drawing some inspiration from Leibniz, developing a theory he called Logical Atomism. How this is related to the Vienna Circle's Logical Empiricism and Wittgenstein's philosophy we will not venture into, except to say that things got even more complicated after the end of the 1800s, though theoretical questions of science had to give way to more urgent matters like world wars and depressions and the turmoil of the twentieth century that followed them.

However, to understand Positivism we have to go back to the beginning of the 1800s and view the state of science then. It was in France that the word "positivist" was first applied to theoretical science - by Auguste Comte. But even with him the word became quickly associated with the putting of science in the service of practical human/social affairs.

For Comte was more interested in using modern science to reorganize society after the period of revolution that preceded his birth in 1798. Indeed, in his later work the quasi-religious character of his motive of simply using the new science for the good of society came out quite starkly, to the dismay of some of his earlier admirers, such as John Stuart Mill. Having a Catholic up-bringing his later work went to the extent of proposing a new system of quasi-religious rituals to go with his idea of a new secular religion.

That this new religion of science was more in the anti-religious spirit of the times than otherwise can be seen in this quote from the Stanford article. "'How,' as Comte would put it in 1848, 'does one reorganize human life, irrespectively of God and king'?" (1851, v. 1, 127; E., v. 1, 100)

But it is Comte's early education in the new sciences according to the modern scientific method that provides the clue to his admiration for modern science and his hopes for being able to use it to the advantage of "humanity". As for his exposure to the best science and scientific minds of the time we note that he attended the most prestigious educational institution of the time, "The École Polytechnique, whose faculty included the likes of Arago, Laplace, Cauchy, and Poisson ... There, he got an education in science that was second to none in all of Europe; it left a permanent imprint on him." (from Stanford article).

He later wrote a couple of books on Geometry and Astronomy. Such was his standing in the scientific community of the day "In April 1826, Comte began teaching a *Course of Positive Philosophy*, whose audience included some of the most famous scientists of the time (Fourier, A. von Humboldt, Poinsot)." (Stanford) He had the credentials for writing on the sciences, which had already developed to be a wonder to the modern world. But he had greater plans than simply expounding them, which he was later to expose in a following book entitled "System of Positive Polity", whose full title was *System of Positive Polity, or Treatise on Sociology, Instituting the Religion of Humanity.*

Though there is evidence that this socio-political motive was present from the beginning, this turn to a kind of humanistic mysticism came as a shock to his most ardent admirers, amongst whom was John Stuart Mill, who was to be regarded as the principal exponent of scientific positivism in the English speaking world of the nineteenth century. However, Comte's was not a turn to religion is any real sense but an exaggerated worship of what already underlay the enthusiasm for modern science.

Intimately connected with this perceived triumph of the human spirit, was the belief that at last man had discovered the means to end the ills and troubles that beset the human condition, or at least alleviate them as never before. No longer need Man be content to regard suffering, hardship and pain as inevitable accompaniments of human life, or have regard for any religion teaching such a lot of humanity as the consequence of sin. (*pace Rerum novarum* n. 18)

Indeed, the possibility of progress in human perfection now seemed assured by science. That state of mind generated by the modern scientific revolution was not peculiar to Comte, if overblown by him, but became enshrined in a belief in inevitable Progress. Therein lay the germ of the charge that religion is the enemy of science, which was taken up by the Socialists and in-

deed is preached to this day by those, who we may call "human-
ists", who hope to "reorganize human life, irrespectively of God
and king".

What is worth bringing out here is that committed individualistic liberalists in theory readily slipped into being socialists in
fact. This was obvious in the case of Comte, but it may be noticed
in John Stuart Mill, and even in going back to Jeremy Bentham,
in the commitment of will to social reform, of society generally
and of the law in particular, according to their idea of what human happiness consists in. We have referred to above how this
voluntaristic/"democratic" philosophy contains the germ of to-
talitarianism.

We do not say much in this book about John Stuart Mill as he
wrote little of any significance about the theoretical side of science. He wrote a book on Logic in line with empiricist thought
that reduced all reasoning to induction. He even considered that
mathematical propositions such as $2 + 2 = 4$ had only a high degree of probability. He was identified mainly with those called the
Philosophical Radicals, members of a movement of ethical and
political import that indeed was most influential in the English
speaking world of law and politics (even into recent times). It became virtually the official philosophy behind the political parties,
first Liberalist or Conservative, and later Socialist or Progressive,
pushing for law and other social reform in all sorts of ways, according to a humanist vision of the world that we have seen in
the early Comte. Mill adopted much the same stance as the early
Comte.

However, we are concerned here not with the practical/political part of Positivism, but with it as a theory of science that derives from Empiricism but survived the failure of Kant to incorporate Hume's empiricism into his theory of knowledge and science. Hume's philosophy of science is irredeemable, for it attempts to base it on sense knowledge alone. His philosophy is already flawed by going along with the idealist presupposition so that the mind is aware first and indeed only of its internal impressions.

He rightly noted that all human knowledge, up to the highest kind, has its beginning in sense, but not sense as idealistically conceived by the empiricist. How is it then that Hume's theory, despite its denial of the possibility of any intellectual or rational truth, and consequentially, the denial of the first principle of non-contradiction (aside from the undermining of this by the idealistic presupposition), was thought not to undermine a positivist notion of science?

The reason we believe is primarily pragmatic, the dramatic success of Newtonian Science. The real advance of modern science that was going from strength to strength could not be denied. Together with this Hume had read the secret of Newton's scientific method as resting in its factual basis, the "laws" of physics, such as of gravitation, if expressed mathematically, came naturally out of observation and experimentation. Hume thought we should be able to discover the most general laws of human nature in the same way. His experimental method had less success than did Adam Smith who, with a subject matter more attuned to the material side of human nature produced "An Inquiry into the Nature and Causes of the Wealth of Nations" and in the process created one of the first of the new modern sciences. Comte envisaged that the same could be done for human nature as a whole, which with prophetic insight he called Sociology.

Though Hume could not defend his position "rationally" it was pointing up the remedying of a deficiency that had developed in pre-modern natural science, of being too "rationalist", and neglectful of the need for continuing observations and experimentation (research), as we have explained earlier. Another way of putting this is that Newton's physico-mathematical science was viewed simply as a sophisticated "Physics", supplanting the old defective "Aristotelian" physics, or Natural Philosophy as it was still called.

There was no notion of distinguishing between pure natural science, pure mathematics and the mixed science of mathematical physics as Aristotle and Aquinas did. Astronomy for them was a different kind of science from Physics. So when Newton's book was entitled "The Mathematical Principles of Natural Philosophy" it was simply taken as the new "Natural Philosophy" with a change of name to Physics.

Pure Mathematics survived relatively intact, but the distinction between physics and mathematical physics became obscured. Indeed, what seems to have occurred is that the mixed method of physico-mathematics as employed by Newton was so successful that it became "the scientific method" and was applied to all known branches of science, so that Science came to be seen as one great endeavour involving observations and measurements applied to all sorts of subject matters newly classified as we know them today.

Comte's classification is an early example of how "Science" was being divided. He listed six fundamental sciences—mathematics, astronomy, physics, chemistry, biology, sociology. It may be seen how the scope of science had been contracted to the mathematical and physical order of reality, with human nature, as social, reduced to the same material level so as to be subject to the same scientific method. Comte as we note saw Sociology also as the organizing principle of the others, reminiscent of Aristotle's comment that if Man were the highest thing in reality Politics would be the supreme science. We have adverted to the sinister socio-political implications of this.

The modern mind could not cope with the diversity of sciences in Aristotle's scheme, which was the more complex the more one descended into the more concrete level of material things. We have described how the scheme may be pictured as a kind of pyramid with Metaphysics at the top, and the unifying principle, Physics at the bottom involving a multitude of different sciences, and Mathematics in the middle.

Mathematics can be viewed as more abstract and formal than the natural sciences and so be used as an organising principle of mixed sciences. This is what deceived Kant. But, as well, mathematical forms being quantitative rather than qualitative are used to organise natural things in a uniform and mechanical way; the rich diversity of natural forms, and our appreciation of their specific worth and beauty, is lost. What is gained is our ability to control nature and its forces, like putty in our hands. This unfortunately was used to the advantage of a few who could use their "capital" (money) to have the worker majority make not just wealth for consumption and circuses, but also weapons for destruction and domination.

However, we will not go any further into this comparison of the Aristotelian and modern approaches to science. We will say some more in our last book. What we wish to bring out here is the fact that the mixed nature and method of modern science is not to be thought false or untrue to reality on account of the false and even absurd philosophical presuppositions that were invented to explain its supposed superiority, but is to be accounted narrow in its this world focus and consequently dispiriting for the generality of mankind.

The physico-mathematical method, if known by Aristotle and Aquinas only in certain specialized forms such as Astronomy and Perspective (Optics), and applied in ways appropriate to the different mixed subject matters is, in essence, a genuine scientific method. Newton applied it so successfully to Astronomy and Optics that it became generalized.

At the same time the empirical side of the natural sciences (now stripped of natural forms unfortunately) was rightfully restored to its essential role in physical science. It too was generalized so as to provide a "matter" for the mathematical treatment of the bodily side of things including human.

By a strange absorption of Kantian thought the problem of not having any certainty from lack of Metaphysics was met by taking on Kant's notion of phenomenon as the object of science, the laws then able to be accounted as hypothetical only, "final" truth able to be put off to some future time.

This turn to founding science on laws and theories as hypotheses was not there at the beginning with Newton. *Non fingo hypotheses* was his famous saying. His principles were regarded as certain scientific truths, and his basic concepts, such as space and time absolute (even eternal properties of the divine). But with the advance in observation and experiment, both at the macro and micro levels, a degree of uncertainty and relativity began to enter into modern science.

So at the turn of the century there was a new revolution in modern science, mention of which we have made above. We will not go into it in this book as it involved a revolution not just in Physics but also in Logic and Mathematics. We will examine it in our last two books, "Logic, Science and St. Thomas Aquinas" and "Natural Philosophy, Modern Science and St. Thomas Aquinas".

We have done enough here to show how modern thought, in its philosophy, undermined the first principle of non-contradiction and the very notion of truth.

Conclusion

This conclusion is called for only because the modern period of science had in one sense not ended at the close of the nineteenth century. That sense is the purely temporal; time and change go on if a particular mode of thinking has essentially exhausted itself. The modern era in this latter sense ended as soon as it began.

Descartes was the beginning and end of modern thought in its defining mode, which was the rejection of the things, substances and accidents, outside the mind in which, as we have explained, were the forms of which the human mind needed to be informed if it was to know anything at all.

The argument raised by Hume was one that did not address the fundamental issue, but simply corrected Descartes's exclusive reliance on imagination and the mathematical order of thinking. The new notion of science as constructed by Newton, from which Hume took his lead, took science at the same particularist level, but as a mixed science of empirical knowledge as well as mathematical. That is still concerned only with the physical order of being that is the object of investigation by Physics and Mathematics, and by Physico-mathematics, as explained. Hume took this empirical level in the same subjectivist/idealist way as Descartes.

The rationalism/empiricism dispute was an in-house one, not affecting the fatal flaw of the idealist presupposition, which cut off the human mind from physical reality (and the world of being) it belonged to. From this followed immediately the rejection of the first principle of human understanding, the principle of non-contradiction. However, we do not wish to go over what has already been dealt with.

It is true that another source is needed to explain human intellectual knowledge and that internal, the light of understanding. This is what Kant may have had some inkling of, but, as a mathematician and mathematical physicist, he could not rise to the necessary metaphysical level, as he openly admitted. Accordingly, he botched the whole nature of human knowledge and only exacerbated the disconnection of the human mind from reality, with which went the first principle of understanding.

However, we should look a little more closely at the effect of Newton on modern thinking. The pre-modern Physics had the problem we have referred to. Newton took advantage of the new discoveries from better observational techniques, but in the context of a mathematical physics, to produce what was taken to be a refutation of the old (Aristotelian) physics (in which Astronomy was tended to be seen as an integral part) and the true explanation of the nature of the real world.

We have explained how mathematical physics is a distinct mixed science, not always easy to distinguish from pure physical science, or mathematical science for that matter (Aristotle had difficulty), but the parts of which were clearly explained by Aquinas in terms of form and matter. Thus, the physico-mathematical sciences are genuine sciences and there is nothing wrong with the mixed scientific method that goes with them.

Newton was not all that concerned with any idealist presupposition, or with the denial of metaphysical principles that that entailed, and so there is in principle no reason to criticize Newton's scientific method. However, he did place too much emphasis on the formal/mathematical side of the science and tended to absolutize the concepts he used.

This led to a determinist interpretation of the laws he formulated which, on more acute modern observations and measurements, were found to need adjustment. What has been called the "New Physics" not only allows for relativity of concepts and uncertainty of laws, but there was a propensity to put relativity and indeterminacy as the very basis of the new view of science. As too often happens in reacting against one extreme, the modern scientific mind has gone to the other of absolute indeterminism and relativity.

As noted, the modern mind is not fazed by radical irrationality, and all sorts of absurd propositions have been boldly put forward, and supinely accepted by a mystified public, as consequences of the "new physics". What happened, however, is that before the New Physics, Newtonian laws were too readily given the distinctness and determinacy of mathematics without taking into account that the science did not have the pure form of mathematics, but had the composite nature of physico-mathematics. As St. Thomas had pointed out, if the medial science was formally mathematical it was substantially natural, so that the laws fundamentally depended upon being in accord with observation.

To obtain the right balance, it was not necessary to adjust the laws of geometry, and relativize everything, as Einstein did, to explain how light in passing a physical body may be observed to deviate, or "bend". The modern mind, as did the pre-modern, tends to think that light is somehow special and different from "matter" generally. But, Aristotle defined it as the activity of something that belongs to the physical world, if he was not too clear as to what it was. There is more to matter than we think, as modern investigations continue to show.

Thus, we may see that the revolution in the science of Physics (Mathematical physics) that occurred at the beginning of the twentieth century was a needed revision of concepts and laws taken too much in the form of pure mathematics. This extreme was corrected, but went too far, in the move to the less formal mode of natural science. Unfortunately, this revision did not know where to stop in taking account of the indeterminacy of matter (and potency), and has tended philosophically to the opposite extreme, as indicated above.

The genuine scientists manage to work without getting too involved in the problems presented by the philosophical errors propagated in the name of official science that is taught in the universities. As may be expected, however, the revision, fundamental as it was, has led to all sorts of changes in philosophical positions, not just in the notion of science as understood in modern thought, but also in the notions of pure mathematics and natural science.

Indeed, the distinctions between these three orders of science are not well understood in modern thought, for reasons that should be clear. Mathematics has had to be looked at in relation to empirical observations and experiment, and what Aristotle regarded as Physics or Natural Science (Natural Philosophy) has to be looked at as empirical "material" for mathematical "analysis" in all sorts of subject matters. The abstruse theorizing that has ensued, particularly in regard to mathematics, has become impossible to follow.

However, we need to note that there was already a revolution in thinking taking place in various modern sciences even before that in Physics. And here the change was of an opposite nature and may be attributed rather to the increase in the domination of Mathematics in what were seen as positive sciences.

The clue to the change may be seen in the addition of the word "logical" to positivism. The more significant of the changes were in the notions of Logic and Mathematics, so that their studies could be referred to as the "New Logic" and the "New Mathematics". There was a great effort by mathematicians such as Russell and Frege to prove that Mathematics could be reduced to Logic, or that Logic could be expressed in the language of mathematical formulas.

Such changes in the understanding of the notions of Mathematics and Logic led on to the invention of the computer. Computing is a mathematical term, but taken at the lowest mechanical level. Here again the "progress" was in the increase of usefulness of science to man at the expense of understanding. The notion of intelligence was reduced to such a low level that serious consideration is being given to human intelligence being surpassed by that of the robots it creates (AI).

There is a close affinity between Logic and Mathematics in Aristotle, but the proper context for discussing the foundations of Mathematics, as of any particular science, is Metaphysics. And logic, being the consideration of method, has to be specially adapted to each particular science, so that mathematical logic is not the same as general logic. But these are topics we will take up more fully in our next book.

What we can say at this stage is that the changes in the treatment of logic and mathematics in most recent times do not essentially change the deficiency in the modern understanding by reason of the failure to take Metaphysics into account. This tends to make much of the philosophical discussion of the nature of logic and mathematics a tortuous process that mostly leads nowhere.

Though many particular thinkers simply concentrate on their own specific subject matter and may implicitly hold to metaphysical principles, their thinking cannot fail to be affected by the "official" position of skepticism taken in regard to science generally. That is not to deny that much truth is discovered despite these obstacles.

However, even before the "New Logic" and "New Mathematics" were coming to the fore the so-called positive sciences were being affected by a greater reliance upon the mathematical side of the scientific method. As we have noted, this theoretical method was applied not only to theoretical sciences, such as Astronomy and Atomic Physics, but also to practical sciences, especially social ones.

A good indication of this is the change in the name of Political Economy to Economics. It is noteworthy that the principal nations involved not just in the new Economics but also in the new Logical Empiricism, were England and Austria, with some involvement by others, such as Sweden. For example, W. Stanley Jevons is a notable name in the context of the new logic and what came to be called Neoclassical Economics (which J. M. Keynes mistakenly called "classical").

The New Economics became so closely associated with the Austrian School of Menger, von Bohm-Bawerk, and von Weiser, later to be followed by von Mises and von Hayek, that it is referred to as Austrian Economics. This became closely connected with the London School of Economics and people like Lionel Robbins, who so defined Economics as to equate it with a science of choice of whatever. "Economics is the science which studies human behaviour as a relationship between given ends and scarce means which have alternative uses" (p. 16 in "An Essay on the Nature and Significance of Economic Science").

At the same time the focus turned to the study of human individual psychology (the object of choices being "subjective" utility) as opposed to the study of the relation between "capital" and "labour" in political terms (perhaps to avoid the growing encroachment of Marxist doctrine, which seemed to take the notions of Capital and Labour in the Political Economy of Adam Smith and David Ricardo "objectively". This was a misreading, as Smith was no doubt as much affected by the idealist presupposition as his close friend David Hume. The terms "subjective" and "objective" were rather used as equivalent to the opposition between individualist and socialist that are at the centre of modern social theory.

In fact, the whole philosophical and scientific scene became hopelessly complicated with the lines of thinking, theoretical and practical, logical and mathematical, psychological and sociological, being intertwined still on the basis of an idealist presupposition and the particularist rejection of metaphysical principles, including the first principle of non-contradiction.

To close we should explain that the injection of Aristotelian concepts and principles, first in the context of human psychology, is traceable to Franz Brentano (1838–1917). We have said something about him above. But his influence upon most recent modern thought has been enormous, as one would expect from a rediscovery of Aristotle. We just list some of modern thinkers who were actually taught by him. Edmund Husserl, Sigmund Freud, Tomas Masaryk, Rudolf Steiner, Alexius Meinong, Carl Stumpf, Anton Marty, Kazimierz Twardowski, and Christian von Ehrenfels.

Unfortunately, the understanding of Brentano of Aristotle was imperfect (as was too it seems his hold on the Catholic Faith. He left the priesthood in protest against Vatican I's declaration of the infallibility of the pope). We can appreciate however the complications introduced into modern philosophy though his influence. He is best known for having reintroduced the notion of intentionality in regard to knowledge.

This was central to Husserl's Phenomenology but was later given a pseudo-metaphysical twist by a student of Husserl, Martin Heidegger (another ex-seminarian). This seemingly theoretical exercise, however, like with Comte and Marx, had a practical/political motive and became a driving force behind postmodernism not only in modern socio-political philosophy but also in modern theology.

However, as we are concerned in this book with the theoretical side of human philosophy and science we do not wish to go into the practical/moral/political (and economic) complications that so plague modern life. They will have to be sorted out, as far as possible, elsewhere.

That will have to do so far as our conclusion of this book is concerned. Obviously, there is much more that could be discussed to indicate the difficulty of dealing with all the complications that have arisen in modern philosophy in recent times. We have compared coping with these complications to eating a stew into which all kinds of lines of modern thought have been mixed together, but trying to digest what has developed since Kant and Hegel might better be compared to trying to eat the thinnest of soup with a fork.